OF GOOD STOCK

BY MELISSA ROSS

DRAMATISTS
PLAY SERVICE
INC.

OF GOOD STOCK
Copyright © 2016, Melissa Ross

All Rights Reserved

CAUTION: Professionals and amateurs are hereby warned that performance of OF GOOD STOCK is subject to payment of a royalty. It is fully protected under the copyright laws of the United States of America, and of all countries covered by the International Copyright Union (including the Dominion of Canada and the rest of the British Commonwealth), and of all countries covered by the Pan-American Copyright Convention, the Universal Copyright Convention, the Berne Convention, and of all countries with which the United States has reciprocal copyright relations. All rights, including without limitation professional/amateur stage rights, motion picture, recitation, lecturing, public reading, radio broadcasting, television, video or sound recording, all other forms of mechanical, electronic and digital reproduction, transmission and distribution, such as CD, DVD, the Internet, private and file-sharing networks, information storage and retrieval systems, photocopying, and the rights of translation into foreign languages are strictly reserved. Particular emphasis is placed upon the matter of readings, permission for which must be secured from the Author's agent in writing.

The English language stock and amateur stage performance rights in the United States, its territories, possessions and Canada for OF GOOD STOCK are controlled exclusively by DRAMATISTS PLAY SERVICE, INC., 440 Park Avenue South, New York, NY 10016. No professional or nonprofessional performance of the Play may be given without obtaining in advance the written permission of DRAMATISTS PLAY SERVICE, INC., and paying the requisite fee.

Inquiries concerning all other rights should be addressed to The Gersh Agency, 41 Madison Avenue, 33rd Floor, New York, NY 10010. Attn: Jessica Amato.

SPECIAL NOTE
Anyone receiving permission to produce OF GOOD STOCK is required to give credit to the Author as sole and exclusive Author of the Play on the title page of all programs distributed in connection with performances of the Play and in all instances in which the title of the Play appears, including printed or digital materials for advertising, publicizing or otherwise exploiting the Play and/or a production thereof. Please see your production license for font size and typeface requirements.

Be advised that there may be additional credits required in all programs and promotional material. Such language will be listed under the "Additional Billing" section of production licenses. It is the licensee's responsibility to ensure any and all required billing is included in the requisite places, per the terms of the license.

SPECIAL NOTE ON SONGS AND RECORDINGS
Dramatists Play Service, Inc. neither holds the rights to nor grants permission to use any songs or recordings mentioned in the Play. Permission for performances of copyrighted songs, arrangements or recordings mentioned in this Play is not included in our license agreement. The permission of the copyright owner(s) must be obtained for any such use. For any songs and/or recordings mentioned in the Play, other songs, arrangements, or recordings may be substituted provided permission from the copyright owner(s) of such songs, arrangements or recordings is obtained; or songs, arrangements or recordings in the public domain may be substituted.

For my sisters. Julie and Kim.

And for Sarah. Fuck cancer.

OF GOOD STOCK was commissioned and first produced by South Coast Repertory, with support from the Elizabeth George Foundation, in March 2015. It was directed by Gaye Taylor Upchurch; the set design was by Tony Fanning; the costume design was by David Kay Mickelsen; the lighting design was by Bradley King; the sound design was by Darron L West; the dramaturg was Jerry Patch; and the stage manager was Kathryn Davies. The cast was as follows:

JESS	Melanie Lora
AMY	Kat Foster
CELIA	Andrea Syglowski
FRED	Rob Nagle
JOSH	Corey Brill
HUNTER	Todd Lowe

OF GOOD STOCK was originally produced in New York City by the Manhattan Theatre Club (Lynne Meadow, Artistic Director; Barry Grove, Executive Producer) on June 4, 2015. It was directed by Lynne Meadow; the set design was by Santo Loquasto; the costume design was by Tom Broecker; the lighting design was Peter Kaczorowski; and the original music and sound design was by David Van Tieghem. The cast was as follows:

JESS	Jennifer Mudge
AMY	Alicia Silverstone
CELIA	Heather Lind
FRED	Kelly AuCoin
JOSH	Greg Keller
HUNTER	Nate Miller

CHARACTERS

The Sisters

JESS — The oldest

AMY — The middle

CELIA — The baby

The Men

FRED — Jess's husband

JOSH — Amy's fiancé

HUNTER — Celia's boyfriend

TIME AND PLACE

A family home in Cape Cod, Massachusetts. Summer 2013.

THE TEXT

A slash in the middle of a line indicates overlapping dialogue.

Internal punctuation inside of a sentence should serve as a guide for emphasis and intention and not be considered true stops.

A beat is a quick shift in thought — a momentary breath — and should not be given *too* much significance. Pauses have a bit more weight. Silences should be allowed to linger.

*Many men have tried to split us up
But no one can
Lord help the mister
Who comes between me and my sister
And Lord help the sister
Who comes between me and my man*

—Irving Berlin

OF GOOD STOCK

ACT ONE

8:30 A.M.

A family home in Cape Cod. The occasional sound of gulls. A breeze through the windows. Jess enters with a basket of vegetables and fresh-cut flowers, presumably from a garden somewhere on the grounds. She is hip-ish and sweet-ish like an older version of your favorite RA from some sort of New England liberal arts college. It is a pretty house. Clean and bright and lovely. It is a house that looks like whoever lives there has never had a bad day. This is a stark contrast to Jess's uniform of stylish casual neutral separates, accented perhaps with a brightly colored pair of Converse. She begins the process of sifting through the vegetables, sifting through the mail, putting things where they should be. Fred enters in old saggy boxers. They might have holes. They might flap open a bit and show off what's going on underneath. He might have a belly that hangs over the top. He inspects a pot of coffee.

FRED. Is this fresh / or is it.
JESS. Ohmygod Fred??? / What the.
FRED. What???
JESS. Put *pants* on! What are / you doing???
FRED. Nobody's here!!!
JESS. Everybody's *gonna* be here / any second!
FRED. Why why why do I haveta dress up for family???
JESS. Would you please just honey please. / Put pants on.

FRED. Oh for fuck's sake fine whatever. *(He exits.)*
JESS. And a shirt too please!
FRED. You got it Mom!
JESS. Ew don't say that! Why would / you say that!
FRED. Relax!
JESS. I'm younger than you!
FRED. Yes yes yes / whatever.
JESS. And I am nothing like your *mother*!
FRED. Then stop acting like her! *(From off.)* Do you have a pants preference?
JESS. Nope.
FRED. Because once I get dressed I'm / not changing.
JESS. NO PREFERENCE!!
FRED. ALL RIGHT! *(She sifts through mail. He reenters in loud madras plaid pants. That look a little old? Maybe? They don't fit so well? He's also wearing an undershirt. He dumps the old coffee out and begins the process of making a new pot. She opens a big envelope with a huge stack of pages.)*
JESS. At what point do you think people will stop trying to turn my father's books into movies?
FRED. Probably never.
JESS. It is borderline harassment. It is environmentally irresponsible. To send this much. Paper.
FRED. Anybody interesting? *(He looks through various canisters.)*
JESS. Some chick who had a hit at Sundance last year. She's like. Twelve. Some director I think I'm supposed to've heard of who I have never heard of.
FRED. You should just do it. He's dead. He can't get mad at you.
JESS. Not my art. Not my choice. *(She gets up to put a pile in recycling and grabs a green juice out of the fridge. She sees him and his plaid pants. She makes a face.)*
FRED. Don't / say it.
JESS. Didn't we throw those pants out?
FRED. You said you / didn't care.
JESS. Haven't we thrown those pants out. *Multiple* times?
FRED. Come on! They're very beachy. They're *cruise wear*.
JESS. Didn't we also discuss a shirt?
FRED. I'm wearing a shirt.
JESS. A *real* shirt.
FRED. I will put on a *real* shirt. When there are people here aside

from *us*. *(Beat.)* You know … When you met me you didn't have an issue with any of my clothes.

JESS. When I met you it was 1987. Those pants were a little less hideous in 1987.

FRED. Minute and unimportant detail. And did we bring more coffee?

JESS. I disagree. And yes it's in the Whole Foods bag.

FRED. *(Checks the bag.)* Found it! They sell Gorilla Coffee now at Whole Foods?

JESS. Yup.

FRED. That makes me a little sad.

JESS. Why?

FRED. It's like when your favorite band has a big huge hit and you suddenly have to share something you love with. People who won't really appreciate it. *(He begins to make coffee.)* You want?

JESS. Nope I'm good.

FRED. You got your "green juice."

JESS. Yup! Mmmmmm … Want one?

FRED. Absolutely not.

JESS. What happened to "the year of Health and Fitness"?

FRED. I have decided instead that it will be the year of Sloth and Gluttony.

JESS. Honey …

FRED. I do not want to drink green juice that looks like bile! I want to eat meat full of nitrates and drink gin and tonics.

JESS. OK.

FRED. And I don't want to have a / discussion about it.

JESS. OK OK I said OK!! *(She opens up an elaborate wedding invitation. An instrumental version of "Just the Way You Are" by Bruno Mars plays. Or maybe "I Love You Always and Forever" by Donna Lewis. Or "You're Still the One" by Shania Twain.* You get the picture. Fred comes over. They both look in awe.)*

FRED. Wow. Is that really happening?

JESS. I think it really is.

FRED. Stop it please. Please make it stop. *(Jess closes the invitation. She opens it again. She closes it again. She puts it away.)*

JESS. This wedding is six months away and it's already annoying.

FRED. Of course it's annoying. Amy had a wedding for her cats.

JESS. I know / but it's.

---

* See Special Note on Songs and Recordings on copyright page.

FRED. She had a wedding. For her cats. As a grown adult person. *(Beat.)* She ask you to be in the wedding?
JESS. Nope.
FRED. That's weird, right?
JESS. I'm fine not being a part of the "wedding of the year". I'm happy to just. Show up as a guest.
FRED. That sounds passive-aggressive and I'm not even the intended recipient. *(Mail sorting. Coffee making. Green juice drinking.)*
JESS. *(Without looking at him.)* Those pants make you look like a douchebag in a teen movie.
FRED. From 1987.
JESS. *(Laughs.)* Yes. From 1987. *(He does an awkward little dance. It's a dad dance. Even though he's not a dad.)*
FRED. *(A spontaneous awkward little song.)* You know you want me. You know you want me bad in my. Plaid. Pants. *(She laughs.)* Dance with me.
JESS. I don't dance.
FRED. You useta dance.
JESS. *(A little laugh.)* In a mosh pit maybe?
FRED. So I'll go put on some. Public Image Limited.
JESS. *(Still laughing.)* Nope.
FRED. Dead Milkmen? / Sex Pistols?
JESS. No! No dancing! *(An attempt that's ignored. He shrugs it off. Coffee drinking. Mail sorting. Green juice drinking.)* Cee's bringing a guy. Did I tell you that?
FRED. *Really???*
JESS. Yup.
FRED. Is it serious?
JESS. No idea.
FRED. Who *is* he?
JESS. I donno. It's just some *guy*. She met him in Missoula.
FRED. When was she in Missoula?
JESS. That Habitat for Humanity trip she did with her girlfriends.
FRED. She is constantly going on assorted change-the-world trips / with assorted girlfriends.
JESS. Do you actually *listen*? When people talk / to you?
FRED. Uh … Sometimes?
JESS. *(A little laugh.)* Well. She went on a trip to Missoula. To build houses. She met him there / I think?
FRED. And what. She brought him home with her?

JESS. I guess. I don't know all the details.
FRED. Well I don't know how I feel about it.
JESS. Honey I don't think how *you* feel is important. To *Celia*.
FRED. I just. I worry about her.
JESS. She's fine. She does this. She loves to take in. Lost things.
FRED. You are only validating my concerns.
JESS. It's not like we know all that much about Josh.
FRED. Amy's different than Celia. Amy probably did a credit check on the first date.
JESS. You're too overprotective of her. She's not even *your* sister.
FRED. I've known both of them since they were kids.
JESS. Listen. You don't have to. Worry. About Cee. She's fine. *(Teasing.)* You're such a good guy.
FRED. No I'm not. I'm a crotchety curmudgeony old man.
JESS. That's what you like people to think / but I know the truth.
FRED. Keep quiet about it. You're gonna blow / my cover.
JESS. *(Laughs.)* Fine fine. *(Beat.)* We should … Figure out dinner.
FRED. I've got a London broil marinating / downstairs.
JESS. I think Celia's a vegetarian? / Maybe?
FRED. Since *when*.
JESS. Remember? She was reading that book about the farming industry? / Last summer.
FRED. Vaguely?
JESS. On and on she went, remember. "I don't judge. I'm not / judging. But."
FRED. Oh jeez. Right.
JESS. She might eat fish? I feel like. Remember she ate a lobster roll? Last time she / was here?
FRED. Kinda?
JESS. Pay attention. You have to / pay attention.
FRED. Is any of this really important?? This *minutiae* of what people eat???
JESS. *(Laughs.)* You're a food writer!!!
FRED. So???
JESS. So that's what you *do*! You *write passionately* about the *minutiae* / of what people eat!
FRED. Indulging the constantly changing food whims of your sisters is *your* job / not *mine*!
JESS. Can't you just pick up some bluefish / or something?
FRED. Ugh why do I have to deal with this???

JESS. Anything on the grill is your jurisdiction, right? Isn't that / the agreement?
FRED. *Preparing* not *purchasing*.
JESS. *(Begging.)* Come on! I gotta go to the store before everybody gets here and the good fish place is in the / opposite direction.
FRED. I told Grayson I'd get him my final draft / by tomorrow.
JESS. OK OK I'll do it / I'll go.
FRED. It's my first national cover story.
JESS. I know! I know! I'm saying I'll do it. / It's fine!
FRED. Woo-hoo!!! Family weekend!!!
JESS. Woo-hoo!!!
FRED. Fun times!!! For all!!!
JESS. My head hurts. I'm already emotionally eating and nursing an imaginary hangover. Whose idea was this again?
FRED. Yours.
JESS. Right.
FRED. I tried to talk you out of it but. As usual. I was *out-voted*. *(Beat.)* It'll be fine just. Keep your expectations low and you might be. Pleasantly surprised.
JESS. All I want is for everybody to play nice.
FRED. Yes well. *That* my dear is what we call a *high* expectation. *(A little laugh from both of them.)* Come on. It's just three days! We can do anything for three days, kid.
JESS. I started getting anxious over a week ago.
FRED. I know. I know. Me too.
JESS. What're you anxious for?
FRED. Because. Like I said. I don't like having to share something I love with. People who won't appreciate it.
JESS. So I'm. Locally roasted coffee beans?
FRED. More like the Pixies. And that is a huge compliment.
JESS. *(A little laugh.)* Yeah. I know. *(Beat.)* I'm sorry.
FRED. *(A laugh.)* For what.
JESS. *(A laugh.)* For being crazy.
FRED. That's OK I. Like me a little crazy. *(A little laugh from both of them.)* Hey.
JESS. Huh.
FRED. Twelve hours till. Somebody's birthday!
JESS. *(Grimaces.)* Oh. Yeah …
FRED. We're almost there kiddo.
JESS. *(Starts to cry but stops herself.)* Uh-huh.

FRED. Hey hey hey. / None of that.
JESS. Right.
FRED. Only celebrating today. OK? *(She nods and smiles. He touches her face gently. A little kiss. Another little kiss. A sexier kiss. They haven't kissed like this in some time, it seems.)*
JESS. Fred … I gotta.
FRED. I miss you. *(His hand finds her breast. She hits him away suddenly and abruptly, almost as a reflex. This takes them both by surprise.)*
JESS. I'm so / sorry.
FRED. It's OK.
JESS. It wasn't conscious. / It was a reflex.
FRED. Sure sure I get it. *(Silence.)*
JESS. You should you gotta. Finish / your article.
FRED. Yeah. I'll uh. I'll. *(Beat.)* Pick up the bluefish! *(A wound that's covered. An attempt at a joke.)* It's the pants, right? Just can't get hot for me in these pants.
JESS. No no. / I'm just I'm not.
FRED. I'll get the mains. You get the sides. K?
JESS. K. *(He looks at her intently. Taking her in. She shyly turns away.)*
FRED. Hey.
JESS. *(Still not looking at him.)* Huh.
FRED. You. You look pretty.
JESS. *(A little laugh.)* Stop it no I don't. / I'm a mess.
FRED. *I* think you … Look. Pretty.
JESS. *(Half-heartedly.)* Thanks. *(They both stand for a minute not knowing what to say next. She goes back to busying herself in the kitchen. He tentatively steps towards her and kisses her sweetly on the back of her head. It is almost paternal. And a little sad. He pours himself a cup of coffee and exits. She turns and watches him leave. She suddenly and without warning vomits into the sink.)*

11:30 A.M.

Celia and Jess. Celia has just arrived and yet it seems she's already everywhere. Open bags. Hair elastics. Tossed-aside shoes. The once-perfect home has been taken over by an explosion of Celia. It is both invasive and also a bit endearing. A lovable mess.

CELIA. Dude! The bunnies! Good god I always forget about the / fucking bunnies!
JESS. I know! They're such a pain in the ass.
CELIA. The pigeons of Cape Cod! Everywhere you go everywhere you turn it's like. "Hey hi! I'm a bunny! I have no sense of life preservation. Look. There I go. I'm in front of your car. Excuse me while I cause an accident! I can't help it! / I'm a bunny!"
JESS. Better than deer.
CELIA. Is it? / Is it really?
JESS. Are you kidding? The *impact* of / a deer???
CELIA. But I mean I almost. Dude! I could've run into you! / Totaled your car!
JESS. But you *didn't*!
CELIA. But I *could've*! I mean. In the grand scheme of things. Better to kill a. Like a. *Bunny.* Than. You know. A *person*?!? But in the moment. You just react. It's like it's. Like a guttural reaction or / something.
JESS. That's *actually* not a word.
CELIA. Huh?
JESS. "Guttural"? I mean yes. It *is technically* a word. But not really correct in this *context*.
CELIA. Ugh. *Dude.* Seriously? Can you stop being such a smartypants for / five seconds please.
JESS. It's not about being smart! It's not a word!
CELIA. You just said it was!
JESS. Well. *Yes.* Guttural. *Is* a word but it's. Referring to a sort of sound? I think *visceral* is the word maybe / you're wanting.
CELIA. No. No it was *guttural*. It was from my *gut*. *(Beat.)* Why can't it be a word if people use it and it's a *good* word?

JESS. Because like mermaids and leprechauns and "irregardless" it does not exist!
CELIA. I think I'm going to use / it anyway.
JESS. Go ahead.
CELIA. Only now I'm gonna be like. *Hugely* self-conscious about it!
JESS. If you want to butcher the English language / feel free.
CELIA. See this is why nobody wants to play Scrabble with you!!! *(Beat.)* For future reference. Like. Later on? When you're like. "Let's play Scrabble!" And it's crickets and tumbleweeds. Now you know. *Why. (Beat.)* Where's the Fredster?
JESS. Working. He's got a deadline.
CELIA. Boo deadlines. Boo. When's Bridezilla Barbie arriving?
JESS. Be nice.
CELIA. I can be a bitch behind her back. That's the family rule. If you aren't here you should assume that everybody is talking shit about you.
JESS. That's *not* nice!
CELIA. *You* made / up the rule!
JESS. *Amy* and *Josh* are arriving sometime after lunch.
CELIA. *(With fake cheerfulness.)* Well isn't that completely not at all vague!
JESS. Cee. / Come on.
CELIA. I'm the flakiest one in the family — and even I was more specific.
JESS. Slightly. *(Beat.)* You want a cocktail?
CELIA. Do we already need an alcohol-induced buzz to tolerate each other?
JESS. A breakfast cocktail! Bloody Mary / or Bellini.
CELIA. I think I'm OK for now.
JESS. The Bloodies are good. We got a black pepper vodka and a little sriracha.
CELIA. That's a very pretentious Bloody Mary. I am so annoyed by that / Bloody Mary.
JESS. Come on! It's delicious!
CELIA. OK. Fine. But no vodka.
JESS. Whadya mean / no vodka?!?
CELIA. I gotta pace myself! We have a whole weekend / of endless drinking.
JESS. OK OK fine. *(She begins to make drinks.)* You useta drink everybody under the table. Remember Gram and Pop Pop's fiftieth?

You drank Manhattans all night and then shots and a champagne toast.
CELIA. And scotch.
JESS. And scotch! And you weren't even a little bit buzzed.
CELIA. I was a college student. I was a professional alcoholic.
JESS. OK.
CELIA. Can't start early and go late anymore. Can't marathon *booze*.
JESS. OK. OK. One Bloody Virgin / for you.
CELIA. Ew! Jess!
JESS. What?
CELIA. Do not call it a. Bloody Virgin! / That's horrible!
JESS. Relax. And one. Yay! Green juice for me!
CELIA. I will drink green juice too! / In solidarity!
JESS. No no let me live vicariously. *(They hold up their drinks.)* Cheers! *(They toast and drink.)*
CELIA. Wow. That's. There is a lot going on in that.
JESS. I put pickle juice from these amazing artisanal pickles I got at Brooklyn Flea. *(Celia laughs.)* What?
CELIA. Dude.
JESS. *What???*
CELIA. Artisanal. *Pickles.*
JESS. That's what they are!
CELIA. Do you even know what "artisanal" means.
JESS. *(Don't be ridiculous.)* Yes.
CELIA. What does it mean.
JESS. *(Beat.)* I mean … I don't know the *actual* / definition of it.
CELIA. All you know is that Fred and his hipster foodie friends told you that it means it's better so it *must* be better, right? Ugh. It's ridiculous. Don't you find it ridiculous?
JESS. What?
CELIA. "I live in Brooklyn. And I drink locally roasted coffee in a BPA free re-usable cup and I eat *kale* that I grow on my rooftop and I knit sweaters made from yarn that I spin myself from the *yak* that I have tied to a tree in / my back yard."
JESS. You can't make yarn / from a yak!!
CELIA. "And I drink small-batch hand-crafted beer that I made myself and I'm serving it along with my artisanal *pickles* and my artisanal *cheese* / and I."
JESS. Point made!
CELIA. "And I pick up my dog's shit in specially made eco friendly

biodegradable plastic bags!" Ugh. Brooklyn wants to be Portland *so bad*. *(Beat.)* Dude. This drink is like. Burning a hole in my esophagus.
JESS. Dude. What's with all the "dude."
CELIA. Whadya mean.
JESS. You've said it like. Ten times already.
CELIA. An exaggeration.
JESS. Also last I checked? I'm not a dude.
CELIA. I don't think "dude" is gender-specific.
JESS. I believe it 100% is.
CELIA. Fine. Shall I call you "madam"?
JESS. Absolutely / not.
CELIA. "Bitch"? "Bitch! This artisanal Bloody Mary is / fucking amazing."
JESS. I just don't remember you talking like Bill and Ted at a Hacky Sack tournament.
CELIA. Why do you care how I talk?
JESS. You are over thirty years old!
CELIA. By whatever by one year!
JESS. Does this guy. Whatshisname? Does *he* say "dude."
CELIA. Sometimes yeah.
JESS. How *old* is he?
CELIA. He is. Age-appropriate.
JESS. Is he a college student?
CELIA. *No.*
JESS. Where is he?
CELIA. He wanted to see a little bit of Boston. So. He's coming later.
JESS. How will he be getting here? Skateboard? / Pogo stick.
CELIA. Bitch!
JESS. Does he have a license?
CELIA. *Yes.*
JESS. *(Laughing.)* Is he old enough to rent a car?
CELIA. I knew this was a bad idea. / Coming here.
JESS. *(Still laughing.)* "Dude chillax."
CELIA. It's a big deal for me to bring him here to / meet you guys.
JESS. I know, love. I know.
CELIA. Even though I haven't known him that long / I still.
JESS. That long??? You've known him for a month!
CELIA. Almost *four months* but whatever. *(Beat.)* This is different, OK?

JESS. Are *you*?
CELIA. Am I what?
JESS. Different? *(A little laugh.)* I mean when was the last time you had a relationship for longer than / six months?
CELIA. I know you think you're the authority on everything and everyone but / you're not.
JESS. I don't!
CELIA. He makes *me*. Different. That's all / I'm saying.
JESS. Well I'm. Looking forward to meeting him. *(Pause.)* Don't get mad Cee.
CELIA. I'm not. / *Mad* I'm just.
JESS. You have a big huge heart. I. Don't wanna see you get hurt.
CELIA. Yeah well. I don't wanna see me get hurt. Either. *(Silence.)*
JESS. *(An attempt at a subject change.)* So! You uh. Get the wedding invitation yet?
CELIA. No why?
JESS. Get ready. *(Jess opens the wedding invitation. The song begins to play.)*
CELIA. I just threw up in my mouth a little.
JESS. It's a lot.
CELIA. Do we have to go?
JESS. *(Laughing.)* Yes!
CELIA. I went to the cat wedding! Why do I haveta go / to this too?!?
JESS. Because! It's your sister!
CELIA. *Is* she?
JESS. Yes!
CELIA. Because sometimes I think she was left on our doorstep and *nobody* ever said anything about it. Don't lie I know you agree.
JESS. Stop it. I love her.
CELIA. Not as much as you love me.
JESS. Cee …
CELIA. Oh for fuck's sake I love her too! I just. Wish I *liked* her more. That's all. *(Beat.)* She said I can't bring Hunter.
JESS. *(Laughing.)* That's his name???
CELIA. Yeah / what.
JESS. Hunter???
CELIA. *(Laughs.)* Fuck you!
JESS. It's so outdoorsy. *Hunter.*
CELIA. Whatever it's a family name. He's close with his family.

JESS. Well that's nice. So are you.
CELIA. *(Laughs.)* Sometimes.
JESS. *(Laughs.)* Sure. Sometimes. I'm. *(Beat.)* I'm glad you're here Cee.
CELIA. Yeah. Yeah me too.
JESS. I'm glad that we're all gonna be. Here. *(Beat. Sincerely.)* Thanks. Thank you for. Not asking me how I'm *feeling*.
CELIA. Oh. I. Jess I. I didn't / mean to *not* ask I just.
JESS. No! I mean it! I really do! I'm so sick of talking / about it.
CELIA. Sometimes I don't know what to say so I. Don't say anything.
JESS. Yeah. Me too. *(Pause.)* Yikes! I gotta get the bags in the car / I forgot the bags.
CELIA. Sorry! We got so distracted! The bunnies!
JESS. Fucking bunnies!
CELIA. Do you need a hand?
JESS. No! No I'm good. I. *(An odd joke.)* Still got both my arms, right! *(She laughs. An awkward beat.)* OK / be right back.
CELIA. Jessie?
JESS. Huh?
CELIA. It's gonna be OK. I promise.
JESS. I mean it'll be / whatever it is.
CELIA. We're Stocktons. Right?
JESS. Right.
CELIA. So ... "We got good stock!"
JESS. Do we?
CELIA. S'what Pop Pop useta say right.
JESS. I guess? *(A little laugh. An odd forced joke.)* So then why do we all just. Keep on dying! *(A sad awkward little beat. Jess kisses Celia on the forehead and exits to get the bags. Celia presses her hands to her forehead — almost as if to hold the kiss close to her before it evaporates. Celia opens the invitation. She listens to the twee little song for a moment. She pounds the card till it shuts up.)*

4 P.M.

Amy, Jess, Josh, and Celia have drinks. Amy is in an outfit. It is her Cape Cod outfit. Not to be confused with her Hamptons outfit or her South Beach outfit. Slightly different from her Nantucket outfit. L.L. Bean tote. Monogrammed. Keds. Khaki skirt. Pastel shirt. Josh doesn't match exactly but. He is definitely coordinated. They are both tan. They are both fit. They both have luggage. Unlike Celia's bags — which are still vomiting over the living room — these are self-contained, managed, and kept in check.

AMY. It is so glorious here!!! Oh my god I forgot. I forget how / *glorious* it is.
CELIA. I know, right?
AMY. The minute the second we drove through Hyannis I said, "Babe. Babe pull over so we can pull the / top down."
JOSH. She hates the convertible.
AMY. I don't *hate* it. It's just. / Too windy.
JOSH. It's cute. She wrinkles her nose.
AMY. *(Wrinkling her nose.)* I do not.
JOSH. See. Like that.
AMY. Stop it!
JOSH. If it weren't so adorable it'd be annoying.
AMY. He's such a tease. Endlessly teasing. *(Jess and Celia exchange a look. Maybe a laugh.)* Anyway so we pulled down the top on the convertible. And I just *sucked* in that luscious salt air. It's so brilliant. It's so glorious. Isn't it babe?
JOSH. *(Teasing her.)* Glorious.
AMY. *(She hits him.)* See what I mean? / See how he is?
JOSH. You love it. She loves it.
AMY. I do not!
CELIA. Wow if you two weren't so annoying you'd be adorable.
AMY. Is that supposed to be funny?
CELIA. *I* think / it's funny.
JOSH. Anyway! It's great to be here.

JESS. You get a lot of traffic?
AMY. None! Can you believe it? / None at all!
JESS. You're lucky.
AMY. I think we made good time. Didn't we babe?
JOSH. Huh?
AMY. Good time. Didn't we make / good time.
JOSH. Oh. Yeah. Yes.
AMY. *(Mock-scolding.)* Men. Never paying attention.
JESS. So funny. I was saying that to / Fred this morning.
AMY. Half of what I say to him goes in one ear and / out the other.
JOSH. Not true!
AMY. What are our wedding colors, babe. *(No response.)* What is *one* of our wedding colors.
JOSH. *(Teasing.)* Is this crucial information?
AMY. See?!?
JOSH. Are they … Lavender and Chocolate.
AMY. *Babe.* They *are*. You *were* listening.
JOSH. You underestimate me.
AMY. I *do*. I take you for granted. *(A kiss.)* Sorry! We're soooo touchy / feely lately!
JESS. It's OK.
AMY. Cee! I feel like I haven't seen you in forever! Right? It's / been forever!
CELIA. It's been a while.
AMY. Was it Christmas? / Is that it?
CELIA. Nope.
AMY. Babe where were we Christmas.
JOSH. Tahiti.
AMY. Right! Tahiti! Wedding plans! How could I forget???
CELIA. Seriously. Babe. How could you. *(Another glance exchange with Jess, who mouths, "Be nice.")*
AMY. Thanksgiving then??? I haven't seen you since Thanksgiving? Could that be right??? / It doesn't seem possible.
JESS. Actually it was when I.
AMY. Babe where were we for Thanksgiving this year?
JOSH. Sofia's.
AMY. Right! Sofia's! / The Hamptons.
JESS. Well whenever it was!
AMY. I swear I have early-onset Alzheimer's! I forget everything / these days.

CELIA. You should take gingko.
AMY. What?
CELIA. Or fish oil.
AMY. Huh?
CELIA. For your *memory*.
AMY. Sure whatever. *(She notices Celia laughing. Is it at her?)* Are you laughing?
CELIA. Ah. / Yes? Maybe?
AMY. *At* me. Are you laughing / *at* me.
CELIA. Oh for Christ's sake / stop it.
AMY. I see you. Making those little faces with Jess / behind my back.
CELIA. It was Jess's surgery! *(Beat.)* That's when we last saw each other. We saw each other when you graced us with your presence. In March for. Jess's *surgery. (Silence.)*
AMY. Oh my god Jessie I. I'm so sorry. I can't believe / I didn't.
JESS. It's OK. Really. I try to forget about / it myself.
AMY. I am a horrible horrible / person.
CELIA. And it's. Back to you!
JESS. It's really fine. I don't expect everybody to be 100% focused on me and / my illness.
AMY. I was going on and / on and.
JESS. I said it's fine. Ame. Really. Let's move on. All right? Who / needs a top-off?
AMY. I didn't forget. You have to know I didn't.
JESS. I know love. Let's just. Drop it. / OK? Huh?
AMY. OK. OK. *(Beat.)* I've just had. *Soooo* much going on. With / the wedding.
CELIA. Is that? Dropping it?
JESS. Cee.
AMY. I have Bride Brain. / All the time.
CELIA. *(Laughing.)* I'm sorry you have *what*??? Is that a real thing??
AMY. Yes it is. It's like Mommy Brain. It's just when you're so focused on your wedding that you become / just you know a little.
CELIA. *(Still laughing.)* Totally and completely self involved???
AMY. *Distracted.* I was going to say / *distracted.* Actually.
CELIA. Uh-huh.
JESS. Josh? Another? / What're you drinking?
AMY. There's a lot to worry about. / With a destination wedding.
JOSH. Uh. Bombay and soda / I think?

JESS. Got it.
CELIA. Right. So much more / important than.
JOSH. And a lime?
CELIA. You know. Fucking *cancer*.
JESS. *(Sharply. Reprimanding.)* Celia. Enough. *(Pause.)*
AMY. It's going to be fun! This weekend. It is going to be so much. *Fun. (Beat.)* I. *(A beat. And then full of sincerity.)* How are you *feeling*. *(Celia begins to laugh again.)* What.
CELIA. Nothing.
JESS. How am I feeling. Uh. *(An attempt at a joke.)* Chemo's a bitch. I throw up all the time. While it kills. Everything inside me but. Other than that I'm. OK!
AMY. Well at least you kept your hair, right?
JESS. Oh. Ha! Actually this? Is a wig!
CELIA. Awesome Amy / really awesome.
AMY. How could I tell? It looks just like her hair. I didn't know. Babe. Doesn't it look / just like her hair.
JOSH. Yeah uh-huh.
AMY. How could I know???
JESS. It's OK! It's whatever. It is what it is. It'll grow back. Unlike my breast! *(Awkward pause.)* Ah. See. I do this. I do this all the / time lately.
JOSH. Do what.
JESS. Make very weird very morbid jokes. That make everybody. Uncomfortable.
JOSH. I'm not uncomfortable.
JESS. OK.
AMY. *(Beat.)* I couldn't tell because it looks so good. *You.* / You look so good.
JESS. Thanks! Thank you! *(Amy starts to quietly cry.)*
CELIA. Oh for / fuck's sake. *(Pause.)*
JESS. Ame. Don't cry lovey. / Don't cry.
AMY. I just I feel so *terrible* / that I didn't know.
JESS. It's OK. Don't be upset.
CELIA. Why are you. / *Crying* about it.
AMY. I'm fine! Just. Pretend / I'm not here!
JOSH. *(Changing the subject.)* So! Uh. Cee. Amy says you got a new guy. Huh?
CELIA. Yeah he's. On his way.
JOSH. *(Begins to comfort Amy with one hand.)* You met him where again?

CELIA. Missoula.

JOSH. Right. Right. And what does he do? *(Amy shrugs Josh away and exits. Nobody responds. This happens all the time.)*

CELIA. What do you mean?

JOSH. Like for a living? / What's his job?

CELIA. Oh! Well he just left school. Actually.

JOSH. Grad school?

CELIA. Uh. No. Undergrad.

JESS. How old did you / say he was?

JOSH. Left? You mean graduated right?

CELIA. Uh. Nope / I mean he.

JOSH. Dropped out?

CELIA. Why is this important. He was in school. And now he is not in school. / Moving on. *(Fred enters. He is wearing the same plaid pants as before. And now he has a Pixies t-shirt.)*

FRED. Hail hail the gang's all here!

CELIA. Fredster!

FRED. Cee! *(She leaps up and hugs him. He lifts her up off the ground.)*

CELIA. *You* are not allowed to work anymore! / You hear me?

FRED. You wanna call my boss?

CELIA. What are you writing about that is soooooo important.

FRED. An interview with David Chang.

CELIA. Oooooh Momofuko!!! / I love Momofuko!!!

FRED. Actually it's Momofuk-U. / Not Momofuk-O

CELIA. How about Momo-Fuck-You? / Does that work?

JESS. It's a cover.

FRED. It's just / a story.

JESS. It's a *national* cover! *(During the above, Amy reenters as if nothing had happened and she'd never left. She resumes her spot next to Josh and settles into the crook of his arm. He gives her a little silent check in. She nods a silent, "I'm fine.")*

FRED. Hey / Ame.

AMY. Hey. Hey.

FRED. Nice to / see you.

AMY. Uh-huh. *(Awkward pause.)*

FRED. Uh ... So! How does everybody feel about bluefish and London broil?

CELIA. I feel solidly OK with that.

FRED. How about your guy? What does he eat?

CELIA. Meat with a side of meat and / a little meat.

FRED. Great I think we got / him covered.
JOSH. All of it sounds great / to me.
AMY. I'll eat whatever. I'm not picky. *(Celia laughs.)* What??? I'm not!
CELIA. Yeah keep / telling yourself that.
FRED. Jess honey what do you want?
JESS. I will eat anything so long as my magnificent chef of a husband cooks it.
CELIA. Aw.
FRED. OK going to the fish market! *(To Jess.)* You're in charge of sides remember?
JESS. Aye-aye captain my captain already / taken care of.
CELIA. Captain my captain. What is that from / I forget.
JOSH. *(Like he's won a game.) Dead Poets Society*!
CELIA. OK. Calm down. / You win.
FRED. Actually it was Walt Whitman. / Before that.
CELIA. Walt Whitman! / Right right!
JOSH. You want a buddy, Fred.
FRED. Ha. Had enough of the Sisters Stockton?
JOSH. *(Laughing.)* Of / course not.
AMY. Don't you dare smoke cigarettes! / Don't you dare.
JOSH. I won't.
AMY. Don't you let him smoke cigarettes Fred.
FRED. I tend to let grown men do whatever they want to do when I'm / babysitting them.
AMY. I mean it Josh. I'll be able to smell it if you do so don't / sneak one in.
JOSH. Aye-aye captain / my captain.
AMY. It's not funny.
FRED. Anybody want anything while we're out?
JESS. Oh!
FRED. Yes …
JESS. Can you go to Marion's pick up a pie?
FRED. So. Two stops?
JESS. *(Begging.)* Please.
FRED. For you. On the day of your birth. My love. Anything. *(He kisses her forehead.)* What kind?

JESS.	CELIA.	AMY.
Strawberry rhubarb.	Boston cream.	Blueberry crumb.

FRED. *One* pie. We're getting / *one* pie.

JESS. Boston cream then. Get / Boston cream.
CELIA. YES!
AMY. I'm lactose intolerant / you know.
CELIA. Since when???
FRED. All right then. / See you all in a bit.
AMY. Since always but. It's fine. / I just won't eat dessert.
CELIA. I thought you weren't *picky*.
FRED. *(In a deep voice.)* Come on Joshua. Let's go do man things. Like. Picking up pies. And *smoking*.
AMY. Don't you dare.
FRED. Hey.
JESS. Huh.
FRED. Four more hours. *(A small shared moment. The men exit.)*
CELIA. Four more hours till what?
JESS. Oh / nothing. Nothing.
AMY. You don't think they'll *really* smoke / do you?
CELIA. Oh for fuck's sake.
JESS. You know. I just wanted to say. / That. I'm really.
AMY. I'm not being a nag. Or a bitch. I'm / just wondering.
JESS. I'm. So happy that. You / guys are here?
CELIA. I'm sure they're smoking / *right now*.
AMY. Ohmygod stop being so *bitchy*.
JESS. I usually don't like to. / Make a big deal about birthdays but.
CELIA. Unfiltered Camels from the second they / leave till they come back here.
JESS. But *this* year. I feel. / Just so grateful that.
AMY. His father died of a heart attack when / he was fifty.
JESS. To have you all here? It / means a lot.
CELIA. So??? *Our father* died in a car accident with a hooker when he was fifty-five. Does that mean you shouldn't ever fuck a hooker / or get in a *car*.
AMY. What is wrong with you???
JESS. *(Struggling to be heard.)* I'm just! This year I am very grateful! *(She has the floor.)* To spend my birthday with you all. *(Beat.)* I mean. I didn't want a production or anything. Or presents. / I just want.
AMY. You *said* no presents. I didn't bring a present because *you* said / don't bring presents.
JESS. No no I don't *want* presents.
CELIA. *I* brought / a present.

AMY. You were emphatic about it. You said. "I'll be very angry if / you bring presents!"
JESS. I DON'T! I DON'T WANT PRESENTS!!! NO PRESENTS! *(Beat.)* I. *(Beat.)* I just wanted. My sisters. Here. For the weekend. I wanted us all to be together. And so it means. So much to me. That you all came. To spend my birthday here with me. In our house? In / this house?
AMY. Well it's actually *your* / house.
CELIA. Ame.
AMY. It's not *our* house. / It's her house.
JESS. It's all of ours. It's *our* house.
AMY. Technically? Not.
JESS. I think of it as *our* house.
AMY. Then why don't you divide it up into three parts?
CELIA. Not / the time.
AMY. I mean if you're really feeling so warm and fuzzy about it. Why not make it right and legit and divide it into three, huh? What's wrong Jessie? You don't / wanna do that?
CELIA. Are you really going to start / that now?
AMY. I'm not *starting* anything. I'm *clarifying*. There is a house. It belonged to our father. He's dead. She owns it. We do not. Right? Am I right? *(Beat.)* Anybody take the room with the ocean view yet?
CELIA. Nope.
AMY. Fantastic. *(She picks up her bag and takes a deep breath in.)* That air, right? It's just. It's so. Glorious. *(She exits upstairs.)*
CELIA. *(Laughs.)* Still "so happy" we're here? *(She refills Jess's drink and clinks with her own.)* Happy fucking birthday.

7:00 P.M.

Josh and Fred are outside overlooking the ocean. They smoke cigars.

JOSH. You're a bad influence.
FRED. Sorry should I take / it back.
JOSH. I mean Cubans? Man. Seriously? / *Cubans???*
FRED. Yeah I know.
JOSH. Where'd you get fucking Cubans???
FRED. Cuba?
JOSH. You went to *Cuba?*
FRED. No. One of my editors went and brought a shitload back for people.
JOSH. So these are *smuggled* Cubans???
FRED. Yeah.
JOSH. That makes them even *better*.
FRED. I know right???
JOSH. I wish I had a scotch. *(They smoke.)*
FRED. Then a scotch you shall have. *(He goes to the car — and comes back with a flask and a cup. Pours a bit for Josh and takes the flask for himself.)* Sorry. Forgot I had this.
JOSH. You got a naked girl in there too?
FRED. Porn on a laptop?
JOSH. Good enough. *(They toast. They drink.)*
FRED. Our apartment's too small for a man cave so. The car is. My domain.
JOSH. I don't have jack shit.
FRED. Sorry.
JOSH. I don't even have a *chair*. Me and the man cat sometimes look at each other and mutually hate our. Emasculated lives.
FRED. That's really. Sad. Josh.
JOSH. Hey at least I don't haveta wear a fucking bell around my neck.
FRED. Yet.
JOSH. *Dick.*

FRED. It's true though.
JOSH. Fuck. Yeah. I mean. *(Beat.)* Yeah …
FRED. *(Another toast.)* To men. To men doing manly
(They drink again.)
JOSH. Technically? She said cigarettes, right? She said smoke cigarettes?
FRED. Oh for fuck's sake. *Joshua.*
JOSH. I know. / I know.
FRED. You gotta man up if you're gonna / make it.
JOSH. Sometimes it's easier to just. Avoid confrontation.
FRED. If you / say so.
JOSH. Do what I'm told.
FRED. You are a grown-ass man. You should *do* whatever you wanna do.
JOSH. You don't get it! Jess is cool. She's a cool girl.
FRED. So's Amy.
JOSH. *(Laughs.)* Come on.
FRED. *(Also laughs.)* What?
JOSH. Cool?!? I mean. Amy's hot. She's super hot and I feel like. She's the one? I mean. I made the / right decision?
FRED. Sure. Sure.
JOSH. But she's not *cool*. Not like how Jess is cool.
FRED. Jess micromanages too. She hates these pants.
JOSH. I gotta be honest. I don't get the pants.
FRED. Come on! They're great pants!
JOSH. They are absolutely *not* / great pants.
FRED. Fucker.
JOSH. Seriously. Get rid of the pants.
FRED. Not gonna happen. I'm gonna die in these pants. And in my will. It will decree. That I shall be buried in them. *(They drink. They smoke.)*
JOSH. She *was* cool. Amy. When we were dating. And then the minute the second I put that ring on her finger. She did a one-eighty. Like. We spent four hours in Crate and Barrel yesterday arguing over *napkin rings*! What the fuck is a *napkin ring*??? It's like somebody ate her brain. Is that a chick thing?
FRED. Napkins rings? I kinda like / napkin rings.
JOSH. *Weddings.*
FRED. Oh. Uh. *(Beat.)* I mean Jess didn't want a wedding. We did the city hall thing.

JOSH. *(Laughing.)* See. I told you. Jess is cool.
FRED. I think I actually would've liked a wedding. A sort of. Public declaration.
JOSH. Well. You can have mine. *(Pause.)* They say you don't really know somebody till year three. *(Beat.)* It makes me kinda nervous. We're only on year *two*.
FRED. Honestly? I've known Jess for. *(Beat.) Twenty-five* years. And I *still* sometimes look at her and. It's like she's a complete stranger.
JOSH. That's. Not encouraging.
FRED. It is what it is.
JOSH. *(Beat.)* So wait. Twenty-five years?
FRED. Yeah.
JOSH. But I thought you just got married recently.
FRED. Not so recent. Seven years.
JOSH. But you've known her for twenty-five?!?
FRED. It took her a long time to figure out that she was in love with me.
JOSH. Apparently. *(Beat.)* So how old was she when you met her?
FRED. Fifteen.
JOSH. How old were *you*.
FRED. Twenty-two.
JOSH. That's slightly illegal Fred.
FRED. No it wasn't like that. I uh. Worked for their dad.
JOSH. No shit.
FRED. Yeah.
JOSH. You worked for Mick Stockton.
FRED. Yup. I uh. Still thought I wanted to write novels. So I was. Taking a creative writing class with him my senior year at Columbia and ... I donno he liked me for some reason. Gave me a job when I graduated.
JOSH. So fucking cool.
FRED. I guess? I wanted to learn how to be a writer. Instead I learned how to be Mick Stockton.
JOSH. *(Beat.)* They're so weird about it. The girls.
FRED. You think?
JOSH. You don't?
FRED. Never noticed.
JOSH. Trust me. They're weird. *(Fred refills Josh's cup.)* What was he like?
FRED. Honestly? *(A little laugh.)* Kind of a dick. Fucking the

maid, the nanny, and the next-door neighbor. While his wife was in hospice.
JOSH. I'm jealous.
FRED. Of what? His virility and questionable code of ethics?
JOSH. *No.* That you got to know him. It's like. It's like meeting. *Salinger.*
FRED. *(Laughs.)* No it's not.
JOSH. I donno. Or like. John Irving. Updike.
FRED. Actually it was more like how you don't wanna work at your favorite restaurant. You know?
JOSH. *(He doesn't actually understand.)* Oh yeah sure sure. *(Pause.)* So. When'd you seal the deal?
FRED. Huh?
JOSH. Jess.
FRED. Ah. Right. Jess. Well. Years later. I'd just broken off an engagement.
JOSH. Oh wow really?
FRED. Yeah. Best decision of my life. But that's a long story. / For another time.
JOSH. OK OK.
FRED. But I read about him dying in the *Times*. *(Drinks. Smokes.)* And there was a picture of the girls. Side by side. Three orphans. Jess in the middle. Holding on to the others. Like she was suddenly the matriarch and I. Hadn't seen her in years but. I donno. Something in me had to. Go and get her.
JOSH. And so you did.
FRED. And so I. Yeah I. Did. *(Beat.)* I *wooed* her. For a whole year. Just hung around till she was ready. She'd say. "You don't wanna mess with me Fred. Cuz I don't want kids and I'm gonna die young." And I'd say. "Neither do I and if you do? I will throw you a kick-ass funeral." *(A pause. They smoke. They drink.)*
JOSH. She doing OK?
FRED. I guess? *(Beat. An attempt at a joke.)* In the words of the great Mick Stockton. "You know you love a woman when you're not fucking her anymore and you keep her around anyway." *(A strange sad pause.)* So ... You uh. Ready?
JOSH. Me? Uh. *(A small sad laugh.)* No. I don't think I'm. I'm not. Ready.
FRED. Don't wanna go back to the ladies / yet huh?
JOSH. Huh?

FRED. Not ready to go back to the ladies?
JOSH. Oh. Uh. Huh. I thought you were. Asking me something else.
FRED. What'd you think / I was.
JOSH. Nothing. Nothing. *(Beat.)* We should. Yes! We should … Go back? *(Beat. He looks out into the water.)* That view is amazing huh?
FRED. Favorite place to be.
JOSH. *(Beat.)* It's almost. Overwhelming.
FRED. The ocean?
JOSH. Yeah … And. I donno. Life?
FRED. Better than death?
JOSH. I mean who knows right? Death might be. Really fucking extraordinary. *(A puff. A drink.)*
FRED. To … Mick Stockton.
JOSH. To Mick Stockton. *(They clink. They drink. They look out into a world that is bigger than they are.)*

8:00 P.M.

The ladies drink. With Hunter. Celia cuts potatoes.

HUNTER. Dude! So wow. I mean. Faneuil Hall is pretty impressive. It's a pretty impressive establishment.
JESS. It's more of a *locale*.
CELIA. Here / we go.
HUNTER. Huh?
JESS. It's not an "establishment" really. It's more of a *locale* or. / A *destination*.
CELIA. Remember what we talked about earlier?
JESS. Huh.
CELIA. *Scrabble. (Beat.)* You want these in halves or quarters / or what.
HUNTER. Anyway I've never been to / Boston before?
JESS. Quarters please / skins on.
HUNTER. And so. It was. You know. Pretty cool just to explore.

Woulda stayed longer but. *(Playfully to Celia.)* I hadda get back to this one! *(He tickles Celia.)*
CELIA. *(Laughing.)* Stop it.
HUNTER. Stop it? Or. *(He tickles her again.)* Don't stop it!
CELIA. *(Squealing.)* Stop it! Hunter please! / I'm going to pee!
HUNTER. Oh all right.
AMY. How'd you get here?
HUNTER. Bus?
CELIA. I told you I was picking him up from / the bus station.
AMY. Are you sure?
HUNTER. Huh?
AMY. That it was the bus? You don't sound? So sure? *(Jess and Amy laugh.)*
HUNTER. Sorry / not following.
CELIA. Ame …
AMY. What??? He said it like a question?
HUNTER. *(Good naturedly.)* Ha. Did I?
AMY. See like that!
CELIA. *That* was a. Genuine question!
AMY. It's not a *bad* thing. / I'm not *criticizing*.
HUNTER. I guess I do? Do that? *(He laughs. Amy laughs.)*
AMY. *(A game.)* Yes yes just / like that!
CELIA. Anyway! He affirmatively positively took the bus / moving on.
AMY. Oh you are no fun.
HUNTER. She's loads of fun! / Are you kidding???
AMY. *(To Celia.)* How does it feel huh? *(To Hunter.)* She and Jess do this to me all the time.
HUNTER. What's that.
AMY. *Tease* me. *Relentlessly.*
CELIA. You're not teasing *me*. You're teasing *him*.
AMY. *(To Hunter.)* Hunter. Do you feel teased?
HUNTER. Nah. I've got twelve siblings. No offense to you guys but. Y'all are amateurs.
AMY. Wait twelve?!? You have / *twelve* siblings???
HUNTER. Yeah my uh. My folks started young.
JESS. Hunter I'm gonna give / you a job OK?
AMY. Twelve? Siblings?
HUNTER. *(To Amy.)* Uh-huh. *(To Jess.)* Sure thing. I love a job. *(Jess brings salad ingredients over.)*

JESS. Nothing fancy. Just cut / and toss.
HUNTER. These from the garden?
JESS. Oh! Uh yes. How'd you know?
HUNTER. I peeked around before I came in. Hope that was OK? / I just.
AMY. You did it again!
JESS. Of *course* / it's OK.
CELIA. *(To Amy.)* Quit it.
HUNTER. The house is just. I mean. Cee told me? A lot about it. But it's. Sorry. Maybe this is weird to say? But is it *really* the house from *Eulogy for* / *a Butcher*?
JESS. Yup.
HUNTER. That book! That book changed my *life* it's. / So amazing!
JESS. Uh-huh. *(Celia hits Hunter.)*
HUNTER. *(Not getting it.)* What? *(Awkward pause.)* So uh. You guys useta spend summers here, right? As kids?
AMY. When we weren't getting shipped off to camp so our father could schtup his many mistresses.
HUNTER. *(Not quite sure what "schtup" means.)* Oh. / Uh-huh.
JESS. It's a *family* house. It was our *grandfather's* before that.
HUNTER. Cool.
AMY. And now it's Jess's!
HUNTER. Oh … / Uh … OK?
AMY. Because our father decided as his final fuck-you to all of us. To leave it / just to her.
JESS. Because he knew that I would take care of it. Because I *was* taking / care of it.
AMY. All right Jess. All right. / It's fine.
JESS. *(To Hunter.)* Those two come once maybe twice a year tops. Fred and I come back and forth all the time / looking after things.
AMY. Because it's *your* house!!!
JESS. You are more than welcome any time / you want!
AMY. As a *guest*! A guest in the house I / grew up in!
JESS. *And* I paid the / inheritance tax on it!
CELIA. It's *our* house! It's our *family* house! Jess just. Is in charge of. What happens to it. / That's all.
AMY. But since she has no kids? If anything happens to her? Our house. Our *family* house. Would probably end up with. Our brother-in-law. / Right?
CELIA. That's not true is it? / Is that true?

JESS. Absolutely not. Can we. Not. Right now? *(Awkward pause.)*
HUNTER. Do you all have like you know a bathroom? That I / could use?
JESS. Of course. / Down the hall to the left.
CELIA. Just use the one in our room. *(Beat.)* Or down the hall / to the left.
JESS. Or the one in your room.
HUNTER. Awesome. I'll uh. I'll figure it out. If I get lost I'll yell!
JESS. Sounds good!
HUNTER. *(Picks up a small backpack. To Celia.)* OK. Just need to. *(Like a fancy lady ...)* Freshen up. *(To Celia. In an odd little voice.)* You're super cute.
CELIA. Aw / come on.
HUNTER. You are! You are super cute! *(He picks her up off the ground in a big bear hug and then puts her down.)* OK I'll be right. Back? *(He laughs. To Amy.)* That was for you.
AMY. *(As he exits.)* See! It's funny. Even *he* thinks / it's funny.
CELIA. Because he's a lovely and sweet person and not an / asshole.
JESS. He's. Older.
CELIA. Huh?
JESS. I don't mean anything by it but he's. Older. Than I thought he was / going to be.
CELIA. I didn't tell you how old he was so why / would you.
JESS. Undergrad? Right? Earlier didn't you say he just / "left" undergrad?
CELIA. So this is about your prejudices? / And your ageism?
JESS. Not saying it's a bad thing! Not weird! Just. I am surprised / that's all.
AMY. *I* think it's weird.
JESS. *Ame.*
AMY. What?!? He's old! He's too old / to be.
CELIA. *(To Amy.)* He's *your* age!
AMY. He's too old to be an *undergrad*!?!
CELIA. He took some time off. To figure out / what he wanted.
AMY. Twenty years???
CELIA. *Seventeen.* / But really.
AMY. Who does that??? Who waits *seventeen years* to / go to college!!
JESS. Amy! Keep it down.
AMY. Oh for Christ's sake he can't hear me!
JESS. The sound echoes! You can hear everything / everywhere!

HUNTER. *(From off.)* Found the bathroom!!
CELIA. Awesome!!
AMY. Does he have a *job*?
CELIA. That is none of your business!
AMY. *Why???* It's a *job*. People have *jobs*. Why can't I ask if he / has a *job*???
CELIA. I just don't feel like talking about it!
AMY. *(Laughing.)* So for how long has he been unemployed?
CELIA. Oh my god! Would you just. Will you just. / Let it go!
HUNTER. *(Reentering.)* Wow! Even the toilet's got a great view!
CELIA. Right???
HUNTER. I mean. Dude! It's like. You're taking a piss and you look to the right and. It's like. Hey! Hi Ocean! How are ya? What's / going on?
AMY. So! You're a fan huh?
HUNTER. Sorry?
AMY. Of our father?
HUNTER. I mean. Uh. *(Looks to Celia.)* I've read some of his books?
AMY. And they. "Changed your life" right? Isn't that / what you said.
HUNTER. One of them did? / Yeah?
CELIA. Amy. Please don't.
AMY. Did you know who Celia was when you met her?
HUNTER. *(Not sure where this is going.)* I mean. No? When we met we were. Building a house? So. *(He laughs.)* I wasn't like. "Hey. I'm Hunter. Could you pass the hammer? Is your dad famous?"
AMY. Of course not. / But when did you.
JESS. *(A save.)* So! Are you … Moving to New York City? *(No response.)* To live near Celia?
HUNTER. Oh! *(Looks at Celia.)* Uh. Didn't you / tell them?
CELIA. I've been waiting till everybody's in / one place.
JESS. Tell us what?
HUNTER. Oh jeez / I'm sorry.
CELIA. It's OK.
JESS. Tell us … What?
HUNTER. Celia's moving. To Missoula.
JESS. *(Beat.)* Oh. *(Beat.)* Well. That's. Sudden.
CELIA. Hunter has. This *amazing* family. / And so.
JESS. What about *your* family?
CELIA. I mean. He's starting a business? / With his dad?
AMY. What kinda business.

HUNTER. Construction?
JESS. Oh. Well that / sounds great.
AMY. You taking a loan out for / this business?
CELIA. Amy!
AMY. What? That's a pretty simple question / to ask.
HUNTER. No it's cool. It's cool. We are taking out a small / loan yes.
CELIA. From *me*. He's taking out a small loan from *me*. That's what you were / wondering right?
JESS. And you are moving to *Missoula*.
CELIA. I'm not moving to. *Antarctica*. It's two plane / rides away.
AMY. That's not the point.
CELIA. What *is* / the point?
HUNTER. Aw. I get it. She's the baby, right? I'm super overprotective of my little sisters too. Don't worry guys. OK? I'll take good / care of her.
FRED. *(As he enters with Josh.)* We have returned from the hunt with provisions for the women! *(He sees Hunter.)* And. One large hairy man.
HUNTER. I'm Hunter.
FRED. Hunter! We've been waiting / for you! Welcome!
AMY. What took you / so long?
FRED. I'm Fred. I'm married to Stockton Sister Number One.
JOSH. We were bonding.
FRED. Whatever he did Ame. / It's my fault!
AMY. Were you smoking cigars???
JOSH. Yup!
JESS. Hey! You smoked those / without me???
FRED. I saved one for the birthday girl.
JOSH. See! I told you she / was cool!
AMY. You smell disgusting.
JOSH. Yup! Isn't it awesome???
AMY. No / it is not.
JOSH. Hey Hunter. Josh.
HUNTER. Hey.
JOSH. I am marrying Stockton Sister Number Two.
HUNTER. Does that make you three?
CELIA. Apparently. This is a / new thing.
AMY. You'll have to come to the wedding, Hunter.
CELIA. You told me he's not invited!
AMY. I *absolutely* didn't / say that!

CELIA. You *absolutely* did!
AMY. I wouldn't ever say that! *(Josh nuzzles into her. To Hunter.)* I didn't say that. *(To Josh.)* I can't deal with the smell OK? / I'm gonna puke.
CELIA. So *is* he invited???
AMY. Of *course* he's invited!
FRED. What're we drinking?
AMY. *(To Hunter.)* Of *course* / you're invited.
CELIA. What *aren't* / we drinking???
HUNTER. Thanks. / Thanks.
FRED. *(To Celia.)* You need a refill?
CELIA. Nah. / I'm good.
AMY. It's in December. The day after Christmas.
HUNTER. Oh. Well I uh. Might haveta spend Christmas with my. Family? / But uh.
AMY. Of course. / Of course.
HUNTER. But thanks. For the. Invitation?
JOSH. Hunter buddy I'm not even sure *I* wanna go so / don't worry about it.
AMY. JOSH!!!!
CELIA. Uh oh …
JOSH. *(Laughing.)* What??? It's not about me. All I really haveta do / is show up.
AMY. It's our wedding!
JOSH. I know! / Our wedding. I know.
FRED. I'm gonna check the grill!
CELIA. But the fun's *just* getting started!
AMY. That's the most hurtful thing / you have ever said!!!
JOSH. It was just a stupid joke!
AMY. *(Begins to cry.)* It's not funny!
JOSH. Come on. Babe …
AMY. Do not "Come on / babe … " me.
HUNTER. *(Quietly to Celia.)* Should we. Go?
CELIA. No. We should pop popcorn.
AMY. If you don't / wanna marry me.
JOSH. Ame would you just.
AMY. Nobody's forcing you! *(She exits.)*
CELIA. Is this the second time she's left crying today? / Or the third?
JESS. Don't.
JOSH. I can't. Deal.

CELIA. *(Slaps him on the back.)* Good luck, dude.
JOSH. I was *kidding*.
JESS. She knows that. It's just. That's Amy. That's always / been Amy.
JOSH. I guess.
JESS. She'll calm down in a minute.
JOSH. This is. My life. *(This is a declaration. And a confession. And a realization. All at once.)* This is. Gonna be. My life. *(A pause. A decision. He stands up. He exits. A car starts up. It drives away.)*
CELIA. Did he just leave?
JESS. I'm … Not sure.
CELIA. Did he just. *Leave* leave.
JESS. He's coming back?
HUNTER. I don't think he's / coming back.
CELIA. Shhhhh! *(Hits him.)*
HUNTER. What???
FRED. *(Reentering.)* OK! So who wants what cooked how.
JESS. I think Josh just. Left.
FRED. Honestly right now all I need to know is if he wants some dead animal and if he wants it still bleeding.
JESS. I don't think Josh is. Joining us for dinner. *(Amy reenters. Fred goes back outside to the grill.)*
AMY. Where's Josh.
HUNTER. He left. *(Celia hits him.)* Would you stop? / Hitting me?
JESS. He went for a drive.
AMY. *(To Celia.)* What did you do to him??
CELIA. What did *I*??? What did *I*??? *Do* to him??? / Are you out of your mind???
AMY. You must've said something!!!
HUNTER. *(To Amy. Defending Celia.)* I think he left / because of *you*.
CELIA. *(To Hunter.)* Stay out of it.
HUNTER. *(Protectively.)* I can't let her talk that way to the mother of my child!
JESS. Woah wait the mother??? / Of your what???
CELIA. He said. In regards to *you*. As you were throwing one of your epic / tantrums over *nothing*. He said.
JESS. I'm sorry did you say?
CELIA. He *said*. And I quote. "This? Is my life." And then he *left*. Cuz clearly the thought / of actually fucking marrying you??
JESS. Did you just say? Did he just say?
CELIA. Was making him freak the fuck out! / So he left your ass!

JESS. Mother of his *child*???? *(Fred reenters.)*
FRED. Hope you / all are hungry!
AMY. *(To Celia.)* What happened to you to make you so / fucking hateful.
FRED. Rare is. Probably just about ready.
JESS. *(To Fred.)* Would you?
FRED. Just trying to move / things along.
JESS. *(To Celia.)* When were you going to tell us that you're pregnant?
HUNTER. Sorry / sorry.
FRED. Wait what who? / Is pregnant?!?
CELIA. I wanted you to meet him first!
JESS. You're having a *baby* and moving to *Missoula*???
AMY. *(To Jess.)* Are you really surprised? She's an alcoholic practically and she's been drinking soda water all night. Plus she's *fat*.
CELIA. Fuck you! / I'm not fat!
AMY. Looks like you're having a *girl*!
HUNTER. *I* think you / look awesome.
CELIA. Well I guess now's as *good a time* as any to tell you that I don't think we're gonna make it to the wedding in *Tahiti* this winter because I'm pretty sure I won't be able to get on a plane! But hey. Looks like it might not happen anyway so. No big deal!! *(Amy grabs a random drink and tosses it at Celia, missing her entirely and getting Hunter instead.)*
AMY. Sorry Hunter.
HUNTER. Oh. Uh. / No worries.
AMY. *(To Celia.)* You. Are *hateful*. *(Amy exits.)*
CELIA. And that makes. Three. Right? Or four? *(Celia starts to cry.)* And you wonder why I'm moving to Missoula? To be with / Hunter's family?
JESS. Cee don't.
CELIA. I'm all fucked up cuz of these fucking hormones and I'm. *Fat*.
HUNTER. You're / not fat.
CELIA. *(Accusatory to everybody.)* Shut up! I am so fat! I'm fucking crazy fat! I'm huge! *(She bursts into tears and exits.)*
JESS. Sorry Hunter.
HUNTER. Oh. Yeah it's OK. I've got seven sisters. And. Six of 'em have been pregnant? So. This? Is nothing. *(Jess hands him a towel to wipe off his face. He does. Beat.)* Family huh?
JESS. Yeah I guess.

HUNTER. I mean. You start out as like. One unit? And then everybody goes off and starts their own unit? And then you gotta like. Work shit out that you already thought you'd worked out. It's weird, you know? Family's so fucking *weird*. *(Beat.)* I'm gonna go / check on her.
JESS. Sure. Sure. *(He exits. Fred and Jess are alone.)*
FRED. Well. We really know how to throw a kick-ass party!
JESS. If by party you mean Armageddon — I would. Agree with you! *(They laugh. A timer goes off.)*
FRED. Ah! Hear that???
JESS. Huh?
FRED. It is somebody's birthday!!!
JESS. Oh yeah … *(Fake enthusiasm.)* Woo-hoo!
FRED. Somebody's forty-one years old. *(An attempt.)* Yay! *(He scurries around.)*
JESS. What're you doing?
FRED. I'm not prepared! *(He puts on a silly hat. And a noisemaker. Throws confetti. Blows a horn.)* Now *that's* a party.
JESS. Sure is. *(She starts to cry but stops.)* I did it!
FRED. You did it.
JESS. I've officially. *(A strange joke.)* Outlived my mom!
FRED. Yeah. Yeah you sure did. *(Beat.)* Happy Birthday, kid. *(They stand far apart from each other in the midst of the mess and the aftermath of the chaos. A quiet and stolen moment alone. He stretches out his hand to her. She stretches out hers to him. They are too far apart to touch. Fred blows the horn again. It's a sad and silly little sound.)*

End of Act One

ACT TWO

10:00 P.M.

Jess and Fred sit outside eating dinner. Alone. Jess is distracted and can't sit still.

JESS. They've been up there for almost an hour and a half.
FRED. I know. Isn't it nice.
JESS. It's weird. It's eerily quiet.
FRED. It's *peaceful.*
JESS. In that way that it gets in a horror movie right before someone gets *killed.* *(Beat.)* Do you think they're OK?
FRED. Not your problem.
JESS. I *know* it's not / my *problem* but.
FRED. Please just sit and enjoy the. Momentary respite. From the chaos of your siblings. *(She sits. They eat.)*
JESS. *(Loud whisper.)* Cee's *pregnant*?!?
FRED. *(Also whispering.)* It appears yes / she is.
JESS. And moving to Missoula!?!
FRED. *(Still whispering.)* We have said this fifty times / already.
JESS. Cee is *pregnant*! And moving / to *Missoula.*
FRED. *(Not whispering.)* No matter how many times you say it / it's still true!
JESS. *(Hits him.)* Shhhhhhhhh!
FRED. *(Whispering again.)* These are all facts so why are / we whispering?!?
JESS. We need to get his Social Security number!!!
FRED. *(No longer whispering.)* Are you / insane?!?
JESS. Shhhhhhhhh! To do a / background check.
FRED. So we know if he paid his taxes??? *(Beat.) You* were the one who was telling me this morning to / mind my business!
JESS. *(Hushing him.)* Would you please keep it down?!
FRED. *(Whispering again.)* You're being crazy!
JESS. No I'm not! It was different when they were just dating! / Now it's.

HUNTER. *(Entering.)* Hey!
JESS. *(Quickly covering.)* Hey hey!
HUNTER. Cee's she's uh. She'll be down / in a sec.
JESS. Oh sure sure!
HUNTER. She's. Embarrassed? I told her / not to be.
JESS. Embarrassed? It's family!
HUNTER. I mean yeah. That's what I said / but she's.
JESS. Should I go get her?
HUNTER. No / she's fine.
FRED. No! / Just sit.
JESS. OK OK.
HUNTER. She'll be. She's coming right. Down. *(Awkward pause.)*
JESS. So! Hunter! You hungry?
HUNTER. Oh. Uh. Should we. Wait? / For the girls?
JESS. No. No. It'll get cold. / We started.
FRED. We're almost done.
JESS. Fred's already / had seconds.
HUNTER. Okey-doke.
JESS. You want some London broil? The marinade's / amazing it's.
FRED. If you like spicy. It's / got habanero.
HUNTER. Whatever you got. *(Laughs.)* I'll eat roadkill if it's cooked the right way. *(Is that a joke?)* Kidding! I mean / kind of.
JESS. Ha ha.
FRED. Roadkill! That's. Hilarious. *(Awkward pause.)*
JESS. I'll make you a plate!
HUNTER. If it's / no trouble.
JESS. Be right back! *(She exits. The men sit alone.)*
FRED. Jess likes to "make a plate."
HUNTER. Well I … Like to eat!
FRED. Good good. *(Beat.)* So! *(Beat.)* Uh … Hunter! You were … Born in Montana, huh?
HUNTER. Oh uh no? I was. Actually born in Virginia. We um. We moved out there when I was seven?
FRED. Huh. Interesting.
HUNTER. Is it? *(Awkward pause. Jess reenters with a plate. Sets it in front of Hunter.)*
JESS. Here you go!
HUNTER. Oh! Wow! That looks delicious.
FRED. There's plenty more where / that came from.
HUNTER. Mmmmmmmm.

FRED. It's good. / Right???
HUNTER. Mmmmm. Hmmmm. *(Jess and Fred watch him eat.)* Are you guys gonna eat?
JESS. Oh no we / ate already.
FRED. I'm stuffed!
HUNTER. OK. *(They watch him eat.)*
JESS. So! Hunter!
HUNTER. Yes! This is all amazing / by the way.
FRED. It's the marinade. / Habanero.
JESS. You said you are one of *twelve*.
HUNTER. Thirteen actually. I have twelve siblings.
JESS. Oh / right right.
FRED. It's got a little kick / to it right?
JESS. Where are you.
HUNTER. Huh?
FRED. The / marinade.
JESS. In the birth order.
HUNTER. Oh! Uh. In the middle. And yeah. Woo-hoo! Spicy!
JESS. Wow right in the middle. You don't say.
HUNTER. Yeah me and my sister. I'm uh. I'm a twin.
JESS. Twins!
HUNTER. Yeah uh. Multiples. Run? In my family?
JESS. *(To Fred.)* You hear that? / Twins!
HUNTER. My aunts are twins. I've got / triplet cousins.
JESS. *(Covering concern.)* Wow!
HUNTER. Yeah so. I've got my fingers crossed!
JESS. For twins. *(To Fred.)* Multiples.
FRED. Yes that's. / What he said.
JESS. So not one baby but two!
HUNTER. Actually I think triplets would be so freaking bad-ass!
FRED. Or three.
HUNTER. You know like. A team!
JESS. You could all get t-shirts!
HUNTER. Right?!? *(Celia enters.)*
CELIA. I'm so sorry / about that.
JESS. No worries.
CELIA. I'm all over the place these days. It's like very intense PMS twenty-four-seven.
JESS. I'll make you a plate!
FRED. *(To Hunter.)* See! What / did I say.

CELIA. I think I want some meat.
FRED. We bought you bluefish.
CELIA. Rare. / Like still bleeding.
FRED. Special trip to accommodate / your food preferences.
JESS. I loved the bluefish honey. The bluefish was magnificent. I am so happy we had bluefish! Hunter how're you doing? You need / more of anything?
HUNTER. Oh I'll uh. Take some more of those roasted potatoes?
JESS. Sure thing! *(Jess exits.)*
CELIA. I think this baby is a total carnivore. I suddenly keep / craving meat.
HUNTER. That's my boy!
CELIA. Or girl!
HUNTER. Or both!
CELIA. Or one! / Just one!
HUNTER. I like it mooing. / I like it bleeding.
CELIA. I know baby. / I know.
HUNTER. *(Lifts up his plate to her.)* Moooooooooo …
CELIA. Uh-huh. Just / like that.
HUNTER. Mooooooooooooo. *(Jess reenters with Celia's plate. And a potato refill for Hunter.)*
JESS. Here we go!
CELIA. Thanks.
JESS. Uh-huh!
CELIA. What's going on with you?
JESS. Nothing!
CELIA. You're acting like Martha Stewart on speed.
JESS. No I'm not!
CELIA. Yes you are!
HUNTER. Almost ready for thirds!
CELIA. Slow down.
HUNTER. Aw jeez / sorry sorry.
CELIA. He eats too fast. / He inhales.
HUNTER. It's cuz I grew up with so many kids you know. If you didn't eat quick somebody would take whatever was left on your plate.
JESS. Well with thirteen kids! God bless your mother!
CELIA. Seriously. I can't imagine anybody willingly doing this thirteen times.
HUNTER. Well *technically* it was only / twelve times.

CELIA. I'm just saying I'm only a few months in and I already think it sucks.
JESS. *(Beat.)* Uh. So! Uh. Where? Are you guys going to live? In Missoula?
HUNTER. I think with / my dad?
CELIA. We haven't / decided yet.
JESS. Oh uh.
HUNTER. He has the space and / with the business.
CELIA. *(To Hunter.)* We're still discussing it.
HUNTER. I / thought we.
CELIA. Can we later? Please?
JESS. Well! Whatever you decide. It'll be good to have family around. / With a new baby.
HUNTER. And we can save money.
FRED. Always good to be thrifty!
HUNTER. I mean. I had a big family. So I want a big family.
FRED. Thirteen?
HUNTER. No! No that's crazy! But I think seven? / Maybe, right?
CELIA. Or two!
HUNTER. Two! / Come on!
CELIA. Or one!
JESS. Well you have got lots! To discuss! *(Awkward pause. They eat. Hunter eats like he's in a race. He cleans his plate.)*
HUNTER. Done!
CELIA. All right / calm down.
JESS. You want more?
HUNTER. I should leave room for dessert. There's / dessert right?
JESS. Yup definitely / dessert.
HUNTER. Pie? Some sort of pie. Love pie. Gotta save / room for pie.
FRED. Who doesn't love pie.
JESS. Actually it's cake. Boston cream pie is / technically cake.
CELIA. Whatever it is!!!
FRED. Hunter did you know that you are the first guy that Celia's ever brought home / to meet us.
CELIA. Ohmygod Fred!
FRED. What??? It's true! You didn't / tell him.
HUNTER. It's a *huge* honor.
FRED. See! It's a good thing!
CELIA. It's not / it's weird!

FRED. I figured you'd told / him already.
CELIA. Nope! Didn't tell him! *(To Hunter.)* Please don't think it's weird.
HUNTER. I don't. It's not that / big of a deal.
CELIA. I'm thirty-one years old. That's so weird. I'm weird. Don't be freaked out that / I'm weird.
HUNTER. I don't I. Think it's sweet.
CELIA. OK. *(Awkward pause.)* Ugh now I feel weird!
HUNTER. Really / nothing's weird.
CELIA. I'm being so weird. / I'm sorry I'm weird.

JESS.	FRED.
No you're not.	Yes you are.

CELIA. I just. I need another minute OK? I'm gonna just take another minute and. Decompress. / Get a breath.
JESS. Whatever you need hon.
CELIA. Sorry / sorry.
JESS. It's OK. It's OK. *(Celia exits. A pause. Fred abruptly stands up.)*
FRED. Oh for fuck's sake! *(He exits. A beat. Hunter and Jess look at each other awkwardly. He returns.)* Kidding! *(Laughs.)* I felt like I needed to make a dramatic exit.
JESS. It's the theme of the evening. *(Fred and Jess laugh. Hunter stands up.)*
HUNTER. *(Very serious.)* Well I don't think it's at all funny.
JESS. Oh. Hunter / we're sorry.
HUNTER. I think actually that. You're all being kind of insensitive? / And so I'm.
JESS. Fuck. Hunter. / We didn't mean to.
HUNTER. And so / *I'm* leaving.
JESS. We're so sorry.
HUNTER. To go ... Wash the dishes! *(He laughs. Jess and Fred begin to awkwardly laugh too.)* Ha ha. I got you!
JESS. Oh you sure did!
HUNTER. I'm leaving / to go wash the dishes!
JESS. To go wash the dishes. Funny. Right Fred?
FRED. That was a good one! *(Hunter begins to clear the table.)*
JESS. Do you / need help?
HUNTER. I got it I got it sit.
JESS. Thanks! *(Hunter exits with dishes. A beat. Back to a whisper.)* I think we should hire a private investigator.
FRED. That's crazy! / You're crazy!

JESS. Shhhhhhhhh. *(Hunter enters for more plates.)* Ha! That was funny. I'm leaving! To wash / the dishes!
HUNTER. I got you huh.
JESS. Yeah you sure did! *(Everybody laughs as he exits again. Back to whispering ...)*
FRED. You're acting insane.
JESS. Then *you* need to talk to her.
FRED. About what?!?
JESS. About what she's *doing* with / her *life*.
FRED. What happened to "stay out of it"???
JESS. This was before Captain Fertility wanted to knock my sister up with a football team. *(Beat.)* She'll listen to you. All you need to do is just. Put a bit of doubt into her head and then her commitmentphobia will take care / of the rest.
FRED. He seems like a really nice guy.
JESS. He's fine / it's just.
FRED. I think *we've* got enough to worry about without you dealing / with this.
JESS. I'm fine. *(Beat.)* We're. Fine.
FRED. *No.* We're ... Not.
CELIA. *(Reenters.)* Whisper whisper whisper.
JESS. *(Quickly covering.)* Hey! You OK?
CELIA. Yes. Yes I / think so.
JESS. *(Clears the table.)* Good good!
CELIA. My emotions are. On a very / thin wire.
JESS. No worries.
CELIA. I cried over a cup of tea the other day. Have no idea why but. I was suddenly struck by the. Poignancy of. Sleepytime tea.
JESS. Sure. / Sure.
CELIA. That little bear in his jammies just. Ripped my heart outta my chest.
JESS. *(Heading to the kitchen.)* Nothing a little dessert can't fix!
CELIA. You want / help?
JESS. Nope! Sit. Talk to Fred.
CELIA. OK. *(Jess exits. A pause.)* I feel like I just walked in on something.
FRED. Kind of?
CELIA. Sorry.
FRED. S'OK.
CELIA. *(Beat.)* She seems good?

FRED. Does she?
CELIA. I mean *healthy*. She looks *healthy*.
FRED. I donno. It's Jess.
CELIA. Yeah.
FRED. So it's. Hard to tell.
CELIA. *(Beat.)* Are *you* OK?
FRED. Sometimes. Sometimes not. *(Beat.)* A baby huh.
CELIA. *(A little laugh.)* Yeah …
FRED. That's. Nice.
CELIA. You think?
FRED. I do. I do. It's about time somebody around here had a kid.
CELIA. *(Beat. A confession.)* I'm a little scared.
FRED. Of what?
CELIA. All of it? I don't feel qualified to keep anything alive. Including myself. / And I.
HUNTER. *(Reenters.)* You ready for dessert???
FRED. Can't wait!
HUNTER. Woo-hoo! Pie!! *(He exits again with dishes. Pause.)*
FRED. I think … *(Beat.)* I think you. Are gonna be a great mom Celia Stockton.
CELIA. *(Relieved.)* Yeah?
FRED. Uh-huh.
CELIA. *(This means a lot.)* Thanks. *(Beat.)* She's. *(Beat.)* Jess is gonna. She's gonna be OK. Right?
FRED. Hopefully?
CELIA. I mean she's already better / isn't she.
FRED. Sure. Sure. *(Fred laughs and ruffles Celia's hair like a little kid. He drinks. He gets up from the table and looks out at the ocean while Celia quietly tries to keep from crying.)*

10:10 P.M.

Jess bustles around the kitchen. Cleaning up. Putting things away. Hunter stands by, not sure what to do.

HUNTER. Can I. Help you? / With anything?
JESS. Nope I'm good!
HUNTER. Come on. Gimme a job!
JESS. No really. / I got this.
HUNTER. I love a job!!
JESS. Absolutely not! Guests aren't supposed to have jobs they are supposed to sit / and relax.
HUNTER. My mom always said, "You cook you don't clean."
JESS. That's a good rule. I like your mom.
HUNTER. Yeah my uh. My mom was. Awesome. *(Jess clocks the "was" but doesn't ask. She hands him a dish towel. He begins to dry.)*
JESS. So! Whadya think of the Cape so far?
HUNTER. Oh I mean it's. So far it's pretty terrific.
JESS. Yeah it is it is. But. *(Beat. A confession.)* I always feel so out of place here.
HUNTER. Why?
JESS. I donno. Everybody's so. New England-y. I wear too much black. I have no patience. And within three days I'm bored to tears.
HUNTER. Cee's like that too. She's always gotta be *doing* something. I'm always like. "Dude. Sit still you know. Look around you. Breathe in the air. Look at the stars." And she's always like. "Yeah OK now what."
JESS. *(A little laugh.)* Maybe it's a New York thing?
HUNTER. Maybe.
JESS. Maybe it's a Stockton thing. *(Beat. A confession.)* I'm taking a meditation workshop at my yoga center. *(He starts to laugh.)* What.
HUNTER. You gotta take a *class* to learn how to sit still?
JESS. *(Laughs.)* I guess?
HUNTER. *(Laughs harder.)* That's so *sad* Jess.
JESS. *(Laughs too.)* It is isn't it.

HUNTER. Yeah. *(The laughing peters off into a slightly awkward quiet. Amy enters. Red-eyed from crying. She's changed into comfy clothes. Hunter gives her a small, forced smile. Jess envelops her in compassion and talks to her as if she is a child.)*
JESS. Hey there lovey. How're you doing. *(Amy shrugs.)* I kept you a plate.
AMY. *(A sniffle.)* I'm not hungry.
JESS. Come on sweetness. / Eat something.
AMY. Did he call? Did Josh call Fred / or you?
JESS. I don't think so no.
AMY. He should've called by now.
JESS. He's just ruminating. He just needs / some space.
AMY. *(To Hunter.)* You're a guy. *(She pours herself a glass of wine.)*
HUNTER. *(Not wanting to be included in this conversation.)* Last I. / Checked? Yeah.
AMY. Do *you* think he's coming back?
HUNTER. Oh / I mean I.
AMY. *(To Hunter.)* You think I'm going to have to cancel the wedding don't you.
HUNTER. I mean. Maybe? You maybe will. / Have to do that?
AMY. Maybe??? You / think maybe???
JESS. Yes this is *not* helping. / Why don't we just.
AMY. I am going to have to cancel my wedding and it will be completely humiliating. Because. *(Begins to cry.)* Because the invitations have already gone out. *(To Jess.)* Did you get your invitation?
JESS. I did.
AMY. Isn't it *wonderful.*
JESS. It is. *(The ding of the microwave.)* And there we go! Plate is ready! *(She hands Amy the plate.)* Now why / don't you.
AMY. I don't want a plate!!!
JESS. All right. / That's fine.
AMY. And I'm *smoking. (She goes to her purse and gets a pack of cigarettes.)*
JESS. OK. / OK.
AMY. And I don't want to talk about it.
HUNTER. Can you uh try? Not to smoke. In front of Celia? *(Amy looks at him blankly.)* Cuz of the baby. *(Amy continues to look at him blankly.)* Thanks! *(Amy continues staring at him.)* Uh. Thank. You. *(Amy exits. A beat.)* Dude's so not coming back.
JESS. Shhhhhhhhhh.

HUNTER. I'm telling you. He had a look in his eye. And it was the look of. "I'm not fucking coming back."
JESS. Well it doesn't really matter what *we* think / though.
HUNTER. I guess.
JESS. It's about the two of them. I mean. *(Beat. A confession.)* Look. Not gonna lie. I don't particularly feel. *Fantastic.* About you knocking up my baby sister three months after / meeting her.
HUNTER. Two months.
JESS. Sorry?
HUNTER. The. Actual? Impregnation? / Was. Two months?
JESS. Whatever! It's fine! You're both adults. You can. Prematurely breed from now till New Year's I don't particularly care. I'm just saying I'm not *thrilled* / but I'm. *(Fred peeks his head in.)*
FRED. Quick question.
JESS. OK.
FRED. Am I supposed to. Acknowledge the crying or. Pretend that I *don't* notice the crying
JESS. I mean is it full-on crying or just like. Quiet pathetic whimpering.
FRED. It's like. Pouting with occasional sound effects.
JESS. I'm gonna say ignore it? But give her like. A little pat on the forearm.
FRED. Got it. *(To Hunter.)* How're you holding up Hunter?
HUNTER. Having a blast.
FRED. Good good. *(As he leaves.)* Hey hon put on coffee.
JESS. If you drink coffee now you're gonna be / up all night.
FRED. *(From off.)* OK Mom! *(A little sigh from Jess. She takes the cake out of the fridge. She begins the process of making the coffee. Hunter watches. Fred walks over to Amy and gives her a tiny pat on the forearm. She bristles and walks away from him.)*
JESS. Wait'll you taste this Boston cream pie. / It's ridiculous.
HUNTER. I love your sister.
JESS. Sorry?
HUNTER. I *love* your sister. I *love* Celia. *(Beat.)* I fuck I. Didn't mean to blurt that out like that / I just.
JESS. Like I said it's not my business.
HUNTER. I just need you to know that I am here for the right reasons. I'm not. Some kinda freeloader / dude whose.
JESS. That's between you and / my sister.
HUNTER. *(Firmly.)* But I'm *not.* *(Beat.)* She *offered* the money. I

didn't ask. I told her I wanted to make a future for her for us / and she said.
JESS. Listen I.
HUNTER. And *she* said that she'd give it to me and *I* said that if she did I wanted it to be a *loan*. Not a *gift*. It's just important. To me. For you to know / that I.
JESS. OK.
HUNTER. That I love her. And I think? I can make her happy.
JESS. Well see. There's the problem. I'm not so sure that any of us Stockton girls can truly *be* happy. I don't think we're. Happy people. So. Give it a try. But. I'm afraid you are likely going to be horribly disappointed. *(Pause.)*
HUNTER. Celia told me you were sick.
JESS. *Am*. I *am* still. Sick.
HUNTER. She said you're getting better.
JESS. Did she? I don't feel better honestly. I just. Cover well. Learned from my mom how to. Die gracefully.
HUNTER. Sorry.
JESS. Nothing you did it's my. Shitty gene pool. *(Beat.)* So glad she told you!
HUNTER. It / wasn't.
JESS. No really. It's great that my mouth sores, hair loss, and puking gave you guys some really gritty deep shit / to talk about
HUNTER. It wasn't like that.
JESS. Trust me. It's my life. And I'm telling you. It's always like that.
HUNTER. The way she talked about you was. One of the things that made me. Start to fall in love with her.
JESS. Well wow! Isn't that / awfully romantic!
HUNTER. I'm just *saying* that I am glad to meet you! That's *all* I just I. *(Jess gathers up the cake and some plates and turns to go. Hunter contemplates and makes a decision.)* My mom was sick too. *(Beat.)* My mom was sick in the same way you are. In the same way your mom was sick.
JESS. Our mom had *lung* cancer / actually.
HUNTER. All I mean to say is. *That's* what we talked about when we met. *(Beat.)* We talked about you. And my mom. And her mom — your mom. And. How much we miss them? And. How much she. *Loves* you. *(Beat.)* You spend so much of your life. Talking about bullshit. Talking about what you *think* people want you to talk

about. And then you meet somebody who right at the beginning. Shows you their whole heart. And it's like. It changes. Everything.
JESS. That's very sweet.
HUNTER. It's / the truth.
JESS. It's also a very. Idealistic and. Naively optimistic outlook on love. On what *long term* love actually *is*. So. *(Beat.)* I'm sorry. That sounds old and jaded and unsupportive. But. Lately? I feel old and jaded and. Unsupportive. And pretending I am otherwise is sometimes. Exhausting. *(Beat. Softens.)* Listen. I know my sister. OK? And commitment is not her *thing*. And so / before you.
HUNTER. I think. You don't know her. As well as you *think* you do. *(A beat. Jess turns and goes outside with the cake and the plates. Hunter lingers behind in the kitchen. Amy is on the porch — standing to the side and smoking. Fred looks out at the water. Celia sits alone. A moment of quiet. Jess pauses in the midspace between the kitchen and the porch. Halfway between this moment she's just had with Hunter and halfway to re-entering the party. She doesn't know where to go or what to do. She almost begins to cry but stops it. A deep breath. Game face. She enters with the cake. It is a presentation. And with it — the momentary tableau is back in action.)*

10:40 P.M.

Dessert and coffee. Outside. Under the stars.

CELIA. Where are the candles??? / You need candles!
JESS. No candles! No singing!
FRED. No singing??? But I wrote a special song / for the occasion!
JESS. No singing!!!
CELIA. Where's Hunter?
JESS. He's / coming.
CELIA. PIE!!!! Hunter!!!
JESS. Well technically it's cake. *(Fred tries to grab her onto his lap and kiss her. She pulls away from him.)*
CELIA. *(To Jess.)* Stop micromanaging my word selection!
JESS. I'm not! I'm just / *clarifying*.

CELIA. PIE PIE! Come out come out / for pie!
AMY. Well. / That's mature.
HUNTER. *(From off.)* Where are the mugs???
FRED. In the cabinet!
CELIA. Do you want help?
HUNTER. Got it!
CELIA. I can help! *(Hunter enters with coffee and mugs.)*
HUNTER. I said I got it.
CELIA. Cream / and sugar.
HUNTER. Cream and sugar. *(He exits.)*
CELIA. Would you just / let me.
HUNTER. Sit! That's an order!
CELIA. All right / all right.
FRED. *(To Celia.)* We like him. *(To Hunter.)* We like you Hunter!
CELIA. Do you? He's great right?
JESS. He does seem to dote on you.
CELIA. *(Laughs.)* It's just cuz I got his baby in me.
FRED. He's a nice guy. Right Jess?
JESS. *(Perky positivity.)* Yes! / Nice guy!
AMY. *(Refilling her own wine glass.)* You know what isn't nice? Not waiting to start dinner until everybody's ready. Just forging ahead and. Stuffing your *pie*holes / while a.
FRED. *(Holding up the pie.)* PIEhole!!!!
AMY. While a family member's world is just. Falling apart / in front of you.
CELIA. There was no clear timeline for when you'd be back!
AMY. *So.*
CELIA. So we were hungry and there was food and you / weren't here and so.
HUNTER. *(Reentering.)* Cream and sugar!
CELIA. And would you please keep your smoking / over there.
AMY. You know what this was like?
CELIA. Please do not say / your sixteenth birthday.
AMY. This is like that time when I was late coming home for / spring break.
CELIA. Here we go!
AMY. On my sixteenth birthday and someone made an executive decision to eat / my cake.
CELIA. I can't believe / we're talking about this.
AMY. Just moved on and ate my cake without me.

CELIA. It is not / remotely like that!
AMY. Who cares about Amy's feelings! Who cares that it's her Sweet Sixteen! We just wanna eat her / fucking cake!
CELIA. Good god! Why does everything have to be / a therapy session???
AMY. Whose idea was it to eat the cake?
CELIA. It was over *twenty* / *years* ago!
AMY. *(Accusatory.)* It was probably *you*.
CELIA. Oh / come on!
AMY. You probably said, "Daddy I want cake." And he immediately felt the need to shove cake / in your mouth.
CELIA. Fine! I'm sorry. I'm so so sorry Amy. I'm so fucking sorry I ate your cake. Your godawful Cookie Puss drenched in lactose lame Carvel cake! I'm sorry I'm so so very very sorry. It is my one true regret of my entire fucking life!!!
AMY. *(Satisfied.)* Thank you.
CELIA. Do you feel validated? / Or vindicated?
AMY. I do.
JESS. Vindicated. I think / it's vindicated.
CELIA. Whatever it is! Can we be done talking about it???
AMY. For now. *(Beat.)* Jess is your landline ringer on? / Is it charged.
JESS. I donno / I think?
AMY. Could somebody check? I'm not sure I get reception / out here.
CELIA. *You* / could check.
FRED. *I'll* check!
AMY. Thank / you.
FRED. Uh-huh. *(He exits.)*
AMY. I just want to make sure that I hear from him / when he calls.
JESS. I know love I know.
CELIA. *(To Hunter.)* According to Amy our father loved *Jess* most because she *looks* the most like him. And *me* most because I *am* the most like him. I.e., a selfish asshole.
AMY. *(A toast to nobody in particular.)* And me … None at all! *(She downs her drink and pours another.)*
JESS. Not true!
AMY. Very true! Half the time I don't even think he remembered my name.
JESS. That's / ridiculous.
AMY. Even Gram and Pop Pop knew it was true. That's why they

left me more money in the will! *(Fred checks the phone in the kitchen. Opens a Tupperware in the fridge and grabs a slice of London broil. Pours a shot of something and drinks it.)*
CELIA. *(To Jess.)* Is *that* true?
JESS. Absolutely / not.
AMY. *(To Celia.)* They didn't tell either of you / but it's true!
FRED. *(Reentering.)* Phone / is charged and in the cradle!
JESS. All right well everybody's dead so. None of it really matters now! *(Silence.)*
HUNTER. Soooo uh. Hey! Question. Why is it actually called Boston cream pie? If it's not a pie. And is it from Boston? / Like originally?
FRED. Oh! I know this actually.
CELIA. *(Laughing.)* Of course you / know this!
FRED. I wrote a piece on regional desserts for *Bon Appétit*.
CELIA. Fred's a food writer. / Not a critic.
FRED. Not just food. / Often food.
JESS. Mostly food.
FRED. Yes well anyway. I do not know the answer to the pie-cake quandary. *But* I would assume it has something to do with it being a custard-based dessert with a *filling*.
HUNTER. Oh yeah. That / makes sense.
FRED. But! I *do* know that. It was invented by an Armenian-French chef. / M. Sanzian.
JESS. I love it when he / talks food.
FRED. In 1856 at the Parker House Hotel. *And.* In *1996*. Along with the debut of the band known as the Spice Girls officially signaling the true end of / the grunge era.
CELIA. *(To Hunter.)* Ugh the two of them are so smart about / everything all the time.
FRED. The Boston cream pie became the official dessert of Boston, Massachusetts.
HUNTER. That was / very informative.
JESS. I thought ice cream. Was the / official dessert.
FRED. No that's New England.
JESS. Oh right!
FRED. And it's not an official anything it's just that New Englanders eat more ice cream per capita than any other / region in America.
JESS. *(To Hunter.)* He wrote a piece about ice cream for *Food and Wine*.

FRED. There's a place in Missoula!
HUNTER. AHH! YES!!! The Big Dipper!
FRED. Yes! Right! / The Big Dipper!
HUNTER. Dude. The huckleberry ice cream. I'm homesick just thinking / about it.
JESS. What's a huckleberry?
FRED. Kind of like / a blueberry.
HUNTER. We had our first date at Big Dipper! / Kind of date.
CELIA. I didn't know it was a date.
HUNTER. *Dude.* Really?
CELIA. Sorry! I didn't! In retrospect now I do!
HUNTER. *(Teasing.)* Wow ask a simple question like. "What's the origin of Boston cream pie" find out that the most pivotal moment of your entire life was. Completely inconsequential to the person you / shared it with.
CELIA. Ask another one ask another one!
HUNTER. *(Laughing.)* Another what?
CELIA. Another question! Ask somebody another question!
HUNTER. *(Laughing.)* Why?
CELIA. It's fun! It's like we're interviewing each other!
AMY. Is that fun?
CELIA. Yes yes it is! It's getting to know each other! Jess you're in the hot seat!
JESS. *(Laughs.)* I'm not sitting.
CELIA. Sit! Sit / in the hot seat!
JESS. Where's the hot seat?
CELIA. Here!!! Sit here!!!
JESS. *(Laughing.)* OK. Are you drunk? / Why are you drunk?
CELIA. No!!! I'm pregnant!
JESS. You're acting / drunk.
AMY. *I'm* drunk!!!
JESS. Ame maybe / you should eat something.
CELIA. I'm just having a manic episode!
AMY. I'm not / fucking hungry!
CELIA. *(To Hunter.)* Ask another question!
HUNTER. Um ... I donno I. Asked what I wanted / to ask.
CELIA. Dude! Stop being a big pooper ask a question.
HUNTER. OK. Lemme think ... *(Pause ...)*
CELIA. Time's up!
HUNTER. Ah! All right. / Um. OK.

CELIA. Don't over-think it!
JESS. *Now* who's micromanaging?!?
CELIA. Shut it.
HUNTER. OK! Got it! My question is … What's the deal with you guys and Massachusetts.
FRED. That's / a very good question.
CELIA. That's a horrible question!
JESS. Is this me? Am I answering?
AMY. I don't understand this game. *(Amy lights another cigarette and pours another glass of wine.)*
CELIA. *(To Amy.)* It's about getting to know / each other.
HUNTER. I mean because you all live / in New York.
AMY. I already know all of you.
CELIA. *Hunter* is getting to know us. *(She coughs dramatically.)* Ugh. Could you please go stand over there. My lungs hurt just / looking at you.
AMY. *(Stands farther away.)* Fine.
HUNTER. And you were raised in New York. So what's the Massachusetts / connection.
FRED. I think it's a very valid question Hunter.
JESS. I concur. OK. So the story goes. Our father is from Massachusetts. And he moved to New York / in the sixties.
CELIA. To go to Columbia!
JESS. I thought *I* was "in the hot seat."
CELIA. We both are! We're both in the hot seat! *(To Hunter.)* I love this story. *(She climbs onto Jess's chair.)* Move over.
JESS. No room!
CELIA. Then I will sit / on your lap!
JESS. Oh jeez.
CELIA. He moved to New York City to hang out in poetry clubs with naughty Barnard girls. Which he did for a few years. And then? He met our mom at Saks!
HUNTER. What's Saks?
CELIA. Saks Fifth Avenue. Very fancy-schmancy department store.
JESS. He had a meeting with *The New Yorker*.
CELIA. They liked one of his stories. And so he had / to get a suit.
JESS. He didn't have a good suit. Even though he grew up very wealthy. In Belmont. Massachusetts.
CELIA. *(To Hunter.)* Very fancy-schmancy suburb.

d no nice clothes because he had left them all behind.
s rebelling.
king a statement of some sort. But he needed a suit.
Saks. And he spotted Mom. / Selling perfume.
was one of those perfume-sprayer ladies. They only
tty girls / to do that.
e asked for a spritz and she said. / *(In a Polish accent.)*
"No! It is for ladies."
CELIA. *(In a Polish accent.)* "No! It is for ladies!" And he said. "All right then. Gimme / a date instead."
JESS. "I'll take a date instead." Was it "gimme"?
CELIA. Maybe? Either / I don't know.
HUNTER. *(Laughing.)* This is clearly an / important detail.
CELIA. Shhhhhhh!!!
JESS. Anyway and so the New England boy married the Polish girl from Brooklyn. Against his parents' wishes.
CELIA. They wanted him to marry this society chick / at Wellesley.
JESS. But they fell in love with Anna when / they met her.
CELIA. Everybody did.
JESS. Which was nice because both of *her* parents were dead.
CELIA. And she had no siblings.
JESS. Neither did he. And so they decided to make their own brood to carry on the name.
CELIA. But then God *fucked* them with three girls …
JESS. Unfortunately. And they set down roots in New York City. But he sent us all to stuffy and horrible New England boarding schools.
CELIA. Except for me!!
JESS. Yes right. Except for the baby.
CELIA. *(Proudly. To Hunter.)* I was an accident.
JESS. *(Laughing.)* More like a surprise.
CELIA. And then he got really famous and emotionally distant. And she was sad and stoic. And then we all lived not-so-happily ever after. Until everybody died. Except for us. The end. *(She hops off of Jess's lap.)*
AMY. *(Beat.)* I think he loved her though.
CELIA. Mom?
AMY. I think in his own way he loved her.
CELIA. In his own way yes I guess so.

JESS. Is there any other way to love someone?
FRED. I love you, Jess.
JESS. Thank you honey.
FRED. In my own way.
JESS. *(Laughing.)* You're drunk.
FRED. I am. But I. Just wanted to say it out loud.
JESS. A need to declare.
FRED. To the world! I love Jess Stockton! In my own way! Even though she kept her name!
JESS. I'm sorry I'm so sorry but I didn't want to be Jess Schlamish. I just couldn't do it. I love you. I hate your name.
FRED. You are forgiven.
JESS. I love you too. In my own way. *(They look at each other. It's hard to gauge if this is a sweet moment or a sad one. Amy starts to cry quietly. Nobody seems to notice.)*
FRED. So! Celia. Is this baby you are having going to carry on the Stockton name?
CELIA. Oh! Uh … We haven't talked about that yet so. I donno? *(To her belly.)* I mean I think technically? I think you're a Walker.
JESS. Well *technically* you're not *married*. *(Amy begins crying harder. Still nobody notices or if they do they don't care.)*
CELIA. Well / not yet.
FRED. *(Laughing.)* Wait your name is Hunter *Walker*.
HUNTER. Yeah. Why is / that weird?
FRED. *(Laughing.)* Is your middle name Hopper? Or Skipper?
CELIA. *(Catching on.)* Or Tripper? Like cuz you trip a lot?
HUNTER. That's true! I'm very clumsy. And I do hunt and walk also. So that / would make sense.
JESS. *(Laughing.)* Or Gatherer??? Like Hunter / Gatherer Walker!
CELIA. Gatherer???
AMY. *(Gets up.)* Fuck all of you!
CELIA. Oh for Christ's sake / calm down.
AMY. My fiancé left me! And I'm. Sitting here. Falling apart. And we're just moving on like / nothing's happened.
CELIA. You're hammered and crazy.
AMY. Sorry I can't just sit here and laugh and chit-chat. About love. And marriage. And *babies*. Sorry if I'm a / little distracted.
CELIA. Wow so just because something shitty is happening to *you* I can't be happy about the wonderful thing happening to *me*??? Really? / Is that how it goes?

JESS. Do you *want* us to talk about it honey.
AMY. I don't know.
JESS. What do you. *Want* us to do.
AMY. *(Crying harder.)* I don't know. *(She turns to go.)*
JESS. Where are you going?
AMY. Dock.
JESS. Do you want / somebody to.
AMY. *(Exiting.)* No. *(She walks down to the docks. A quiet moment. Nobody knows what to do. Jess stands up.)*
FRED. Sit. / She's fine.
JESS. I feel terrible.
FRED. It's not always your responsibility to fix it. / Or coddle her.
JESS. I *know* that. / I *know* it's not.
FRED. She said she doesn't want anybody following her.
JESS. I just want to make / sure that she's.
FRED. Fine. *I'll* go.
JESS. *You* don't need to coddle *me*. I'm not / gonna break.
FRED. I'm not *coddling* you I'm. Being a participant in this family. Can I do that? *(Beat.)* I know the drill. I'll bring her a glass of scotch. All will be good. *(He kisses the top of Jess's head and exits into the house.)*
JESS. And one for me!
FRED. *(From off.)* That's my girl! *(Reenters with a bottle of scotch and a few glasses. Pours one and hands it to Jess.)*
JESS. Wow you went straight for the good stuff, huh?
FRED. It's a "good stuff" kinda night. You want, Hunter?
HUNTER. Nah I'm good.
FRED. Suit yourself. *(He pours two glasses and heads out to the dock.)*
JESS. Wait. I'm going.
FRED. Will you just let me / take care of.
JESS. Will you just let me take care of myself. *(Beat.)* Gimme one of those glasses. *(He gives her the scotch. To Celia.)* Are you coming.
CELIA. *(Petulantly.)* No. *(A pause. A shift between them.)*
JESS. OK.
CELIA. I'm just / sick of.
JESS. I said OK. *(Jess exits to the dock. Silence.)*
HUNTER. So! Who has another question! *(Celia gets up and exits into the house.)* Or … Not. *(Hunter and Fred sit together in awkward silence.)* Scotch offer still on the table?
FRED. Yup.
HUNTER. Are they. Always like this?

FRED. *(A little laugh.)* Yup. *(Fred pours a glass for Hunter and toasts. The two men sit and drink. Fred pats Hunter on the back in solidarity.)*

11:11 P.M.

Amy sits at the edge of the dock finishing up a call and a cry. Jess stands a bit away — holding the two glasses of scotch.

AMY. Uh-huh. Yeah OK. *(She looks up — sees Jess — and then looks back away.)* OK. OK. *(Beat.)* OK. *(She hangs up.)* Whadya know. 11:11.
JESS. Was / that Josh.
AMY. Make a wish.
JESS. Is / he OK?
AMY. Make a wish! *(Pause.)* You got one?
JESS. Yup. *(They both close their eyes and wish. Eyes open. Pause.)* Was that Josh?
AMY. I thought I told you not. To follow me?
JESS. Is / he all right?
AMY. Didn't I? Didn't I ask that?
JESS. Maybe? I uh. *(Beat.)* Brought you a scotch? *(No response.)* I figure whether you want company or not you won't turn down a glass of Dad's forty-year-/old scotch.
AMY. What do you want.
JESS. Just making sure / you're OK.
AMY. I'm OK!
JESS. Are you / sure?
AMY. *Yes. (Beat.)* Sorry for. Ruining your party.
JESS. You didn't *ruin* anything. We. *(Beat.)* We were all being insensitive.
AMY. Oh that's OK I'm. Used to it by now. *(Beat.)* You can't fix this.
JESS. I'm not trying to.
AMY. Sure you are. Ever since we were kids you. Follow. Me and Cee around like we're your. *Ducklings.*

JESS. I / do not.
AMY. No matter how many times we try to run away from you. We can't get too far. You're always *right there*. Fixing. Doting. Smothering. Your poor little. Motherless sisters. *(She holds out a hand for the scotch.)* One of those is mine? *(Jess hands her a glass. Amy takes it.)* Thanks. *(Silence. They drink.)*
JESS. Can I come sit?
AMY. *(Shrugs.)* It's your house. You can. Do whatever you want. *(Jess sits next to her. They dunk their feet in the water. They sip on their scotch.)*
JESS. We should have a boat.
AMY. *You* can / get a boat.
JESS. We have a *dock*. We should / have a *boat*.
AMY. What we *should* do is sell it.
JESS. The dock?
AMY. The dock the house the / whole thing.
JESS. I can't do that.
AMY. Fine whatever / Jess fine.
JESS. I love this house.
AMY. Ugh. I *hate* this house.
JESS. How could you / hate this house???
AMY. All I see everywhere I look is *Diane*.
JESS. Ugh Diane??? / Ugh. Why.
AMY. It's all her stuff. All her awful bland mediocre / Midwestern stuff.
JESS. It's not so bad.
AMY. It's not us! She threw out everything that reminded her of Mom — including some things that were really / special to me.
JESS. Like what.
AMY. It doesn't matter *what. Specifically.* It's all. Gone. *(Beat.)* She wasn't nice. She didn't want us around. *(Beat.) You* don't know. *You* were in college. *You* never came home. But. For me and Cee? The three summers we had a stepmother were really. Horrifying. *(Beat.)* I ran into her at a Pilates class in SoHo. She had a really bad facelift. *(They both laugh.)* We should sell the house and let somebody make a movie out of one of the books.
JESS. I will be doing neither / of those things.
AMY. Come on! Those books are our legacy! And we're not *doing* / anything with them.
JESS. I'm not selling the rights to the books!
AMY. Fine! Then sell the house!

JESS. No! / Absolutely not!
AMY. It's a pain in the ass and far away. And whenever we're here it's a disaster.
JESS. Believe it or not? I actually *like* seeing you.
AMY. If that were *really* true Jess? We both know we'd see each other more often when we. Live in the same city.
JESS. *(Beat.)* I love you Ame. You / know that.
AMY. I know. *(A laugh.)* In your own way. *(She finishes off her scotch.)* You should've brought the bottle. *(Pause.)*
JESS. Our *parents* are. In that ocean.
AMY. Their *ashes* are in that ocean.
JESS. I can't sell the house when they are both / out there!
AMY. Good god. He's been dead for almost ten years and you *still* need to be the favorite!
JESS. I do not!
AMY. Sure you do! So wherever he is he can see sweet obedient Jess doing *exactly* what he wanted till the day she *died*, right? You win!
JESS. I don't *want* / to *win*.
AMY. Took care of his house, check. Babied his books? Check. Married the guy he hand-picked / for you.
JESS. *(Laughing.)* He did not / hand-pick Fred.
AMY. When're you gonna live your life for *you*? *(Pause.)* Fuck. Someday *I'm* gonna be dead and. Also in that ocean probably and. What will be *my* legacy? Huh? Being the *daughter* of somebody who did something great?
JESS. It's OK to be just a regular person you know.
AMY. *(Laughs.)* Yeah well. I can't even manage *that*. My father won a Pulitzer Prize. I can't even seem to. Procreate. *(She points to her stomach and whispers.)* Apparently I've got *rotten eggs*.
JESS. Aw Ame / I'm sorry.
AMY. What does it matter anyway. Looks like I don't have a baby daddy anymore so. Que sera fucking sera. *(Pause.)*
JESS. *I* wasn't the favorite. *Cee's* the favorite.
AMY. No it was you. It was close. But it was you. *(Beat.)* I think he just *liked* you best. As a *person*.
JESS. Well you were *Mom's* favorite.
AMY. Who knows. I barely remember her.
JESS. You *were*. I used to get so. *Jealous.* The way you'd always cuddle up in bed with her and talk and talk. Like old friends. *(Beat.)* You look just like her.

AMY. I know.
JESS. You're like her twin.
AMY. *(Beat.)* Yeah well. I guess that's *my* legacy, huh? I get to look like my. Beautiful. Dead mom. *(They dunk. They pass Jess's glass back and forth. Silence.)*
JESS. I think I'm gonna leave the house to Cee's baby.
AMY. Do what you want. / It's your house.
JESS. I think Dad and Pop Pop would be happy / with that.
AMY. With a *baby*? With leaving the house / to a *baby*???
JESS. You just said you hated this house!
AMY. Doesn't mean I don't *want* it! Doesn't mean I want it to / go to a.
CELIA. Want what to go where? *(Celia stands at the end of the dock wrapped in a blanket. Nobody responds.)* Want what / to go where.
JESS. Nothing.
CELIA. Nobody ever tells / me anything.
AMY. Jess is leaving the house to your *baby* in her will.
CELIA. Oh really??? That's awesome!
JESS. I'm not / dead yet!
AMY. I thought I said that I didn't want anybody to come / after me.
CELIA. Move over.
AMY. So how'd I wind up / with *two*.
CELIA. Move over! *(She fits herself in-between them.)* I brought the bottle of scotch!
AMY. Thank *god*. *(Celia refills both glasses.)* Where's the oldest undergrad in America.
CELIA. I left him back at the house. Sometimes he's way too needy.
JESS. Because it would be so much better if he ignored you.
CELIA. That's not / what I.
AMY. How long do you really think things are gonna last / with this guy?
CELIA. It's different this time!
AMY. You will be through with this poor love-struck puppy in less than six months. / Only this time.
CELIA. Not true!!
AMY. Only *this time* he will owe you *money* and you'll have a / baby together.
CELIA. That's not gonna happen!

AMY. Oh it is most definitely going to happen, munchkin. It is sooooooo happening. You know it. You know it as much as *I* know that I'm not getting married in Tahiti this winter. So. Suck it up and. Embrace that shit. *(She takes Jess's scotch.)* I am. *Wasted.*
CELIA. You / think?
AMY. I know I'm not *pregnant.* And I know I don't have. *(Whispers.) Cancer.* But. My *fiancé* just left me so. You know what?
JESS. What.
AMY. Tonight? I WIN! *(She drinks.)*
JESS. We don't know that he / left for good.
AMY. Yes! Ha! Yes! Actually we *do* know!!! Because … Wait for it … Josh got into a car accident!!! / Isn't that great????
JESS. Oh my god! Is he OK???
AMY. Oh he's fine. He totaled his stupid rapidly-approaching-midlife-crisis *sportscar* — but apparently the rest of him is just *fine.* He's at Cape Cod Hospital in Hyannis.
JESS. What happened?
AMY. He was *drinking.* And he hit a. *Deer. (Celia laughs.)* Not funny.
CELIA. A little funny.
AMY. Not / at all funny!
JESS. Well thank god nobody's hurt!
AMY. I didn't say that!
JESS. Well the *deer* / is hurt.
AMY. Mindy McAllister is hurt!
JESS. *(Beat.)* Who is Mindy McAllister?
AMY. Who knows??? Some *whore.*
JESS. Oh / Uh.
AMY. They found my number in his "in case of emergency" card that I force him to carry. They said he's sleeping it off. They said there was a "Mindy McAllister" with him. Do I know her? *She* may have a *broken rib* but. *She* doesn't have an "in case of emergency" card" in *her* wallet. So. Can I call *her* family?
JESS. I'm sure there's some sort / of explanation.
AMY. *(Starts to laugh.)* Isn't that hilarious? Or ironic???
CELIA. Ironic how.
AMY. That my *fiancé* got into a *car accident* with some random *bimbo* that he either met at a bar or *purchased* on the internet??? Come on! You don't get it??? *Dad* gets it. *He* thinks it's hilarious. Right Daddy? Just like you! Would be a kick-ass plot point in one of your books! That no matter how much of my life I've spent trying

to meet someone *not* like you I ran right smack into a carbon fucking copy?!? I think it's so ironic it's *delicious*.
JESS. Maybe he was just giving her a ride home. Maybe he was just a. Good Samaritan.
AMY. *(A little laugh/cry.)* Yeah. Maybe. Jess. Maybe. *(Pause.)*
CELIA. He's a fucking douche.
JESS. Cee!
CELIA. What??? It's true!!! / He's a douche!!!
AMY. You hardly knew him!
JESS. He's not dead!
CELIA. I *know* him well enough to know that he's a *douche*! Come on! I know you all think he's a douche whether you say it out loud or not. I mean. He thinks nobody can tell? But he's got fucking *hair plugs*!
AMY. *(A little laugh.)* Ohmygod! Cee!
CELIA. Dude's got fucking Barbie head! *(Amy laughs harder.)* Dude's got fucking armpit hair growing out / of his HEAD!!!
AMY. *(Laughing.)* Stop it! That's so mean!!!
CELIA. Fucking pit head! *(Jess starts to laugh too.)* See what you did Dad? You left a legacy of fucked-up chicks. With men issues.
JESS. I'm not fucked up.
AMY. Of course you are!
JESS. How am I / fucked up?
CELIA. *You. You* are fucked up because you are judgmental.
AMY. YES / YES YES!
CELIA. And … You never allow yourself to feel your feelings!
JESS. That is / completely ridiculous.
CELIA. You are fucked up because you are always *fixing* people.
AMY. *(Happily playing along.)* Oh! Yes she is! / Yes you are!
CELIA. *And* because you take care of everybody else more than / yourself!
AMY. And you're a food pusher!
JESS. Why is this suddenly / all about me???
CELIA. *(To Amy.)* And *you're* fucked up.
AMY. Yes yes do me!
JESS. You've both lost / your minds.
CELIA. Because you care too much about what other people think of you. And you're too sensitive.
AMY. *This* / is true.
CELIA. *And* you're a narcissist!

AMY. Woah I / wouldn't.
CELIA. And *I* am the most fucked up of all!!! Because I have severe *attachment disorder* as a result of not being breastfed *and* because my father disrespected women! So … Fuck you Mom!!! / Fuck you Dad!!!
AMY. I am not a narcissist!
CELIA. Fuck you cuz I'm so fucked up and it's your / fucking fault!!!
JESS. Shhhh …
CELIA. *(Pours the scotch into the ocean.)* Here you go Dad. A little drink for you.
JESS. That's a two-thousand-dollar bottle of scotch!
CELIA. That is completely offensive. I am embarrassed for this scotch.
JESS. Fred's gonna / kill me.
CELIA. Fuck Fred!!!
JESS. *(Laughing.)* Shhhhhhhh …
CELIA. You hear that Fred? Fuck you!
FRED. *(From far away.)* Yeah fuck you too!! *(All three break out into hysterics.)*
AMY. Fuck Josh!
CELIA. Fuck Dad fuck Fred / fuck Josh!
AMY. Fuck Josh! Fuck cancer!
JESS. I am trapped in / a bad movie.
AMY. Come on Jess / Fuck cancer!!!
JESS. Standing on a dock with my sisters cathartically saying / "fuck cancer."
AMY. Say it say it!
JESS. While an easy-listening / chick pop singer underscores.
CELIA. Come on Jess / fuck cancer!!!
AMY. Fuck cancer!!!
JESS. Fine fuck cancer!!!
CELIA. There you go! Feels / amazing right?
JESS. Fuck you fucking cancer you piece of shit!!!
CELIA. Cancer? You are a motherfucking asshole!
AMY. Fuck Mindy fucking / fucking whore!
JESS. Fuck cancer fuck cancer / fuck cancer!!!
CELIA. Fuck everybody in the whole fucking world!!!
AMY. Mindy McAllister I hope you die you fucking bitch / twat asswipe whore!!!
CELIA. Fuck her!! Fuck this bottle of fucking scotch! Dad? You loved this bottle of scotch more than you loved … Amy! *(She laughs.)*

AMY. *(Laughing.)* Fucking fucked up scotch! Fuck you scotch!
JESS. Fuck you fucking fucked up / sick genes! *(Celia pours more of the scotch into the ocean.)*
CELIA. Here you go Dad! Here's your / fucking scotch.
JESS. Wait! We gotta give Mom something. / What're we.
AMY. YES YES! MOM!!
JESS. What're we gonna / give Mom???
CELIA. Yes Mom Yes!!!
AMY. Diamonds!!! We should give / Mom diamonds!
CELIA. Yes! Yes! Diamonds for Mom!
JESS. Where are we / gonna get diamonds?
AMY. For you Mom! *(Amy suddenly and as if out of nowhere throws her engagement ring into the water.)* You can have my fucking three-carat emerald-cut platinum diamond-/covered engagement ring!!!
CELIA. Amy you just.
AMY. Fuck you Josh!!! And fuck your fucking ring! And fuck Mindy McAllister you fucking whore! Fuck Mom fuck Dad fuck my fucking wedding in Tahiti that I didn't want anyway! Fuck my fucking issues!!! Fuck my fucking fiancé!!! / Fuck you Josh!!!
CELIA. Fuck you Josh!
AMY. You selfish fucking Barbie Head. / Fuck you!
CELIA. Fuck you Josh!
AMY. Fuck Josh fuck Mindy fuck Mom fuck Dad fuck cancer! Fuck you cancer! Fuck fuck fuck you cancer! Fuck you for taking my mom! You hear me? Fuck you for leaving me without my mom! And fuck you for taking. *(Starts to cry.)* You can't have Jess!!! You hear me??? You can't have her! Fuck you Dad. I know you loved her most but you can't have her! You hear me? / You can't have her!
JESS. Amy honey.
AMY. *(Brushes her hand away.)* You can't have her!!! Because I cannot I will not lose anybody else! So fucking death fucking Grim Reaper??? Next time you want someone??? Take me. OK? *(Begins fully sobbing.)* OK? Because if you take. One more person that I love. Away from me. I. I am not gonna make it. So don't. Please don't take my sister. Away from me. Please don't. Please please don't. Please / please don't.
JESS. I'm not. *(Beat.)* I'm not going anywhere.
AMY. Make me a promise you can keep. *(Silence.)*
CELIA. You just threw a. Diamond ring. Into the ocean.
AMY. Yeah yeah I did.

CELIA. That's. Fucking awesome.
AMY. Yeah?
CELIA. Fucking. Awesome. *(Amy's sobs slowly turn into an almost laugh. A laugh/cry. They all stand looking out into the ocean. Arm in arm. Celia wraps them up in the blanket on each side.)*

8:30 A.M.

The quiet of early morning. Fred is in the kitchen alone. In good spirits. Humming a bit. Making pancakes. Frying bacon. Brewing coffee. The bustle of breakfast. Jess enters still sleepy in PJs. She hasn't put on her wig yet — and has a pretty scarf covering her head.

FRED. Morning!
JESS. Morning. *(He hands her a coffee.)* There are so many wonderful smells. I don't know what to focus on first.
FRED. Bacon?
JESS. Yes please. *(He hands her a slice. She nibbles. Coffee drinking. Pancake making.)* Bacon is a beautiful thing.
FRED. *(Singing.)* We love you bacon! / Oh yes we do!
JESS. Shhhhhhhhhhhh … You'll wake everybody up.
FRED. *(With excitement!)* I can't wake anybody up because … There's nobody here!
JESS. Where'd everybody go?
FRED. They took a field trip to Hyannis to deal with the. *Josh* situation.
JESS. *Oh* … Right. *That. (Beat.)* I strangely forgot about that.
FRED. Yeah well. It's a situation. There was a lot of crying. And anger. And then more crying.
JESS. Understandably.
FRED. I don't know if he's coming back? Or not? Or I mean. How *awkward* is it gonna be if he *does* come back?
JESS. *Right?*
FRED. It was all. Very stressful so. I decided to cook and. Eat my feelings! You are welcome to join me.
JESS. I will absolutely join you.

FRED. You want a green juice?
JESS. Nah I think I'll stick with bacon.
FRED. That's my girl. *(Bacon eating. Coffee drinking.)*
JESS. *(Whispers.)* Do you think that woman is a *prostitute*?
FRED. *(Also whispering.)* Probably.
JESS. *(Still whispering.)* What was / he thinking?
FRED. *(Still whispering.)* Why are we whispering? Nobody's here.
JESS. *(Laughing.)* I don't know. *(Beat.)* Was he acting strange?
FRED. When?
JESS. When you went out on your little man-date / together.
FRED. Oh! Uh … / I donno?
JESS. What did you guys talk about?
FRED. Lots of stuff …
JESS. Why are you being so cagey?
FRED. I'm not being *cagey* / I'm just.
JESS. Yeah you kind / of are.
FRED. I mean I donno we talked about your dad / a bit.
JESS. Yes and.
FRED. And we … Talked about. You.
JESS. *(Beat.) Me?* What did you tell him / about *me*?
FRED. Nothing! Just. How we met and when we started dating / and we.
JESS. *(A new idea.)* Wait did you tell him about leaving Margaret Patterson at the altar!
FRED. Here have some more bacon.
JESS. Oh my god / *did* you???
FRED. I mean I maybe I mentioned that I had been engaged to someone / else maybe.
JESS. FRED!!!
FRED. WHAT???
JESS. Why would you say that to him???
FRED. Why *wouldn't* I??? It's *my* life. It is something that happened *to me*. And so I should get to tell / whoever I want to tell!
JESS. I *know* that but still.
FRED. How was I supposed to know he was going to find it. Inspiring. *(Beat.)* And for the record. I didn't leave Margaret Patterson at the altar. It was a mutually agreed upon decision.
JESS. *(Beat.)* I think your mother still has hope that one of these days you'll realize that you made a terrible mistake and beg Margaret Patterson to take / you back.

FRED. Stop it.
JESS. *Margaret Patterson* would've taken your name.
FRED. She also would have driven me completely *insane*. *(Beat.)* Listen to me. If he's having doubts. The best thing that could happen to her is that they call off / this wedding.
JESS. I know I know.
FRED. On the Richter scale of tragedy. This thing with Josh is on the low side comparatively.
JESS. *(Beat.)* Right. I mean. It's not *cancer*. *(Pause.)* Isn't that what people always say? When something *really* shitty happens? Like. Hey — sorry your house got broken into but. At least it's not *cancer*. Yikes! So sorry you / lost your job but.
FRED. Why are you always making jokes about it.
JESS. I'm not. Making *jokes* / I'm just.
FRED. Yes. You are.
JESS. *(Beat.)* Well. That's the rule when you're sick. You get to talk about it however you wanna / talk about it.
FRED. But we don't. Actually. Talk about it. *(Beat.)* We don't talk / about it *ever*.
JESS. Can we please just please / not now.
FRED. You go out on the dock with your sisters and I am sitting far away listening to the three of you and all I can think is. I'll bet *they* are a part of this in a way that *I* am not allowed / to be.
JESS. Fred come on.
FRED. Maybe if I took *your* name, huh? Maybe if I was a *Stockton* I could get to feel like I am actually a member of your family and not just some guy who lives with you.
JESS. *Wow*. I'm. *(Beat.)* I'm sorry. I don't. I don't know what to say to that. / I don't.
FRED. Anything! Just tell me whatever's in your head / right now.
JESS. I *can't* I.
FRED. Whatever it is whatever you're thinking / just say it.
JESS. Fine. If you must know if you really want to know. Right now right this second I am thinking that if something happens to me that. That I *hope*. You'll look after my sisters. Because you'll be the only family that they have left. I'm thinking will you take over my dad's estate because that's what *he* would / have wanted.
FRED. Jess I.
JESS. I'm thinking of how to set things up so that. So that you will still be taken care of the way I want you to always be taken care of.

I'm thinking about how I never had kids and I wish I'd had a kid. Why the fuck didn't I ever / have a kid.
FRED. Don't do that to yourself.
JESS. Don't do what? Don't *feel* bad?
FRED. That's not what / I said.
JESS. So what. I can't feel bad. I can't make jokes. You want to tell me what I *can* do? *(No response.)* You wanna tell me how I. How I can. *Be sick.* In a way that feels *acceptable.* / To *you*?
FRED. That's not fair.
JESS. Fair? Wait so now I have to be fair? Make sure that *your* feelings about *my* illness are given / equal weight.
FRED. That's not what I meant! I'm just. We could. We could try for a kid / or adopt a kid.
JESS. This isn't about having a *kid*, Fred!
FRED. I *know* that! / I'm just saying.
JESS. You don't know what it's like to lose your mom when you're young. And while there's still a. A risk of / that happening I.
FRED. OK OK.
JESS. I can't ignore that. Possibility. To just to. To leave something behind if I. Fuck if I. If I *die*. / I can't do that.
FRED. You're not going to die!
JESS. I might! I might still die!
FRED. We can't go there!
JESS. If you want to talk about this. If you really want to talk about it. Then you have to. Fuck. *Allow. Death* to be a part of the conversation! I could die a month from now. I could die six months / from now.
FRED. So could I! Any of us could / die at any moment!
JESS. It is not the same! And how dare you pretend that it is! *(Pause.)* I can't be with you. Really truly present. With you. Again. Until you accept *that* / part of me.
FRED. That you are gonna die???
JESS. That I *could die*!
FRED. I don't I. *(Beat.)* I can't. *(Beat.)* I'm sorry / but I.
JESS. Well then how can you ask me to share it with you? *(Pause.)* Every time I look at your face. All I can see is your worry and. And your fear. And all I can think is how. Is how. *Guilty* I feel that you're. / That you're.
FRED. Hey. Would you.
JESS. That you're stuck. With *me*. *(Silence.)*

FRED. Look at me. *(Shakes her head no.)* Come on. Jess. Look at me. *(She doesn't.)* All I see. When I look at you. Is a beautiful fifteen-year-old girl I knew. A long time ago. *(Beat.)* And all I can think is. How lucky I am. That I somehow convinced the truly extraordinary Jess Stockton. To marry me. *(She looks at him. Really looks at him. She begins to cry.)*
JESS. *(A confession.)* I'm not. I'm not ready. To die.
FRED. You're not / going to die.
JESS. Please don't.
FRED. You are not going to die. *Tomorrow.* OK? Will you just. Will you let me have. *That.* (*Pause. Smoke. Smoke alarms.)*
JESS. Ohmygod / something's burning!
FRED. Shit fuck the bacon.
JESS. Put it in / the sink!
FRED. You do the smoke detector / I do the bacon.
JESS. OK OK OK. *(Fred puts the burning bacon pan into the sink and runs water on it. Smoke everywhere. Jess gets out a ladder and fiddles with the smoke detector.)*
FRED. You gotta take the / battery out.
JESS. Yes yes I know!
FRED. In / the back!
JESS. Fuck yes I know!
FRED. Just take the whole thing off / the wall!!!
JESS. I'm trying! / I'm trying!!!
FRED. JUST TAKE IT OFF THE / FUCKING WALL!!!
JESS. All RIGHT!!!! *(She pulls at the smoke detector until it falls off the wall and onto the floor. Quiet. The end of chaos. They laugh.)*
FRED. I think you ... *Murdered* the poor smoke detector.
JESS. *(Laughs.)* I didn't / mean to.
FRED. *(Very serious.)* We should have a moment. To thank the smoke detector for years of. / Loyal service.
JESS. Honey I.
FRED. Shhhhh ...
JESS. Wait are we really / doing this?
FRED. Close your eyes please. *(She does. He does. They both stand — having a quiet moment for the dead smoke detector, trying not to laugh. She opens her eyes and looks at him.)*
JESS. Are we / still?
FRED. Shhhhhhh ... We are gathered here today to remember Smokey. *(A laugh from Jess.)* And to thank him for his years / of service.

JESS. His? It's a *male* / smoke detector.
FRED. Yes. Thank you Smokey.
JESS. Thank you Smokey.
FRED. Amen.
JESS. Amen. *(Slight pause.)* I gotta say honey. I feel like that was a very underwhelming funeral.
FRED. It was impromptu.
JESS. You better raise the bar for me. That's all I'm saying.
FRED. *(Pause.)* I promise you. That if I need to. I will throw you. A kick-ass. Funeral.
JESS. *(Beat.)* Thank you.
FRED. Anytime, kid. *(He goes back to the sink to deal with the burnt bacon in the pan. She stays on the ladder. Pause.)*
JESS. You. *(Beat.)* You are my. Best friend. You know that? Like. I used to hate it when women said that about their husbands. I used to think that meant they were. Co-dependent? Or bragging. But. *(Beat.)* Lately I've been. Making these. *Lists.* Constantly. Obsessively. Lists of my life. Of. All the people I've ever known. All the people who will come to my funeral. All the things I've done and have yet to do. All the people I'll miss if I die — if you still miss people after you die. The people I'm missing right now. And you. You were the first person I thought of. On every single list.
FRED. You don't have to miss me.
JESS. I know.
FRED. I'm here.
JESS. I know.
FRED. I'm right. Here. *(They stand far apart. She still on the ladder. He by the sink. He reaches out towards her but touches space. She reaches out towards him but touches space. He takes an almost hesitant step closer to her. She steps off of the ladder and onto the floor. They tentatively each reach a hand towards each other. Their fingers touch. Perhaps the far away and distant sound of everybody returning. Jess and Fred's tentative touch turns into something more deliberate and almost desperate. They grasp each other like life preservers. They hold on tight.)*

End of Play

PROPERTY LIST

Basket of vegetables and fresh-cut flowers
Mail
Pot of coffee, mugs, cream and sugar
Big envelope
Manuscript
Canisters
Green juice
Whole Foods bag
Gorilla Coffee
Elaborate wedding invitation
Coffee cups
Bloody Marys, bottles of wine, bottle of expensive scotch, cocktails
Cigars
Flask
Dish towel
Silly hat, noisemaker, confetti
Dinner: salad, roasted potatoes, London broil, Boston cream pie
Pack of cigarettes and lighter
Cellphone
Blanket
Engagement ring
Pancakes
Burning bacon
Ladder
Smoke detector
Cordless phone

SOUND EFFECTS

Song playing in wedding invitation
Gull sounds
Timer going off
Microwave "ding"
Smoke alarm

NEW PLAYS

★ **A DELICATE SHIP by Anna Ziegler.** A haunting love triangle triggers an unexpected chain of events in this poetic play. In the early stages of a new relationship, Sarah and Sam are lovers happily discovering each other. Sarah and Nate know everything about each other, best of friends since childhood and maybe something more. But when Nate shows up unannounced on Sarah's doorstep, she's left questioning what and who she wants in this humorous and heartbreaking look at love, memory, and the decisions that alter the course of our lives. "Ziegler (who makes origami of time)… digs beneath the laughs, of which there are plenty, to plumb the pain that lurks below." –*Time Out (NY)*. [2M, 1W] ISBN: 978-0-8222-3453-1

★ **HAND TO GOD by Robert Askins.** After the death of his father, meek Jason finds an outlet for his anxiety at the Christian Puppet Ministry, in the devoutly religious, relatively quiet small town of Cypress, Texas. Jason's complicated relationships with the town pastor, the school bully, the girl next door, and—most especially—his mother are thrown into upheaval when Jason's puppet, Tyrone, takes on a shocking and dangerously irreverent personality all its own. HAND TO GOD explores the startlingly fragile nature of faith, morality, and the ties that bind us. "HAND TO GOD is so ridiculously raunchy, irreverent and funny it's bound to leave you sore from laughing. Ah, hurts so good." –*NY Daily News*. [3M, 2W] ISBN: 978-0-8222-3292-6

★ **PLATONOV by Anton Chekhov, translated by John Christopher Jones.** PLATONOV is Chekhov's first play, and it went unproduced during his lifetime. Finding himself on a downward spiral fueled by lust and alcohol, Platonov proudly adopts as his motto "speak ill of everything." A shining example of the chaos that reigned in his era, Platonov is a Hamlet whose father was never murdered, a Don Juan who cheats on his wife and his mistress, and the hero of the as-yet unwritten great Russian novel of his day. [9M, 4W] ISBN: 978-0-8222-3343-5

★ **JUDY by Max Posner.** It's the winter of 2040, and the world has changed—but maybe not by much. Timothy's wife has just left him, and he isn't taking it well. His sisters, Tara and Kris, are trying to help him cope while wrestling with their own lives and loves. The three of them seem to spend a lot of time in their basements, and the kids are starting to ask questions. This subterranean comedy explores how one family hangs on when technology fails and communication breaks down. "This smart, disturbing comedy is set…just far enough in the future to be intriguingly weird but close enough to the present to be distressingly familiar… Posner's revelations about this brave new world… waver between the explicit and the mysterious, and each scene… gives us something funny and scary to ponder." –*The New Yorker*. [3M, 3W] ISBN: 978-0-8222-3462-3

DRAMATISTS PLAY SERVICE, INC.
440 Park Avenue South, New York, NY 10016 212-683-8960
postmaster@dramatists.com   www.dramatists.com